M000286756

REVIVAL NOW

HISTORY IS IN THE MAKING FOR THE NEXT GREAT AWAKENING

MAY GOD BLESS

YOU NOW

& ALWAYS!

REVIVAL NOW

HISTORY IS IN THE MAKING FOR THE NEXT GREAT AWAKENING

PETER DE JESÚS

DE JESÚS
MINISTRIES

Some De Jesús Ministries (DJM) products are available at discounted pricing for specific quantities purchased for educational needs, premiums, and sales promotions. For detailed information, email DJM at info@dejesusministries.org.

REVIVAL NOW: History is in the Making for the Next Great Awakening by Peter De Jesús

Published by De Jesús Ministries
P.O. Box 75, Lancaster, Texas 75146
www.dejesusministries.org

Copyright © 2020 by Peter De Jesús
All rights reserved.

International Standard Book Number: 978-0-9966564-2-9
E-book ISBN: 978-0-9966564-3-6

This book or parts thereof may not be reproduced in any form, stored in a retrieval system, or transmitted in any form by any means – electronic, mechanical, photocopy, recording, or otherwise – without prior written permission of the publisher and author, except as provided by United States of America copyright law.

Scripture quotations marked NKJV are taken from the New King James Version ®. Copyright © 1982 by Thomas Nelson, Inc. Used by permission. All rights reserved.

Scripture quotations marked NIV are taken from the Holy Bible, New International Version ® NIV®. Copyright © 1973, 1978, 1984, 2011 by Biblica, Inc.®. Used by permission of Zondervan. All rights reserved worldwide.

Scripture quotations marked KJV are taken from the King James Version of the Bible.

Internet addresses are taken from web sources containing corresponding content at the time of publishing. The author nor the publisher are responsible for any possible changes that may happen at these internet addresses after publication. Additionally, the author nor the publisher possesses any influence or responsibility over the referenced websites and their content.

Printed in the United States of America

DEDICATION

In an era in which the mental health of ministers is now more important than ever, this book is first dedicated to those ministers who have battled and will battle depression. Secondly, in a decade in which a fresh spiritual revival is greatly needed, this book is also dedicated to the remnant of revivalists who believe a great revival is rapidly approaching. Thirdly, in a year in which racial reconciliation is gravely missing, this book is likewise dedicated to the multiethnic Body of Jesus Christ that is willing to unite to usher in the next Great Awakening. Lastly, in a time during which the greatest harvest of souls is ready to be received into God's kingdom, this book is also dedicated to the multicultural Christian community that is committed to sharing the gospel of Jesus Christ with a severely wounded world in grave need of His great salvation.

ACKNOWLEDGMENTS

In addition to God's divine intervention in my life, this book became a reality due to the direct and indirect contributions of some of the most amazing people I know, and others I have not yet met.

To begin with, I want to express my deepest appreciation to our triune God for His faithful work in my life, family, and ministry. I glorify Him for His irrevocable gifts and calling.

Secondly, I profoundly thank my wife, Mildred, our children, Gabriella, Samantha, and David, and my parents, Roberto and Carmen, for their steadfast love, encouragement, and support. I am beyond blessed to have them as my family, my partners in ministry, and as those who have believed in me throughout all the highs and lows in life and ministry. A very special thanks goes to our first-born, Gabriella, who edited this book for me.

Thirdly, I am forever grateful for Senior Pastor Dr. John Hagee and Lead Pastor Matthew Hagee of Cornerstone Church, in San Antonio, Texas. Their love, leadership, and living legacy have impacted my life, family, and ministry beyond words can explain. I count it a great honor to be one of their ordained ministers of Cornerstone Church.

Fourthly, I greatly appreciate the Cornerstone High School Youth and College and Career Ministries' staff members, who, from 2008 through 2013, served alongside Mildred and me. Pastor Michael Fernandez, Pastor Nino Gonzalez, and Worship Leader Bryan Apodaca are some of the most amazing servant-leaders and world-changers I have ever known.

Fifthly, although I only personally know Evangelist Dr. Chris Hill, I sincerely would like to thank him, Pastor Jentezen Franklin, and Pastor Elbert Smart for collectively being used by God to recommend me to Pastor Matthew Hagee, during his national search for a High School Youth Ministries Director and Youth Pastor in 2008. It is amazing to see how God sovereignly provides divine confirmation for kingdom decisions and assignments.

Sixthly, Mildred and I are so thankful for our De Jesús Ministries' board members who are also some of our dearest friends. Pastors Michael and Lucy Fernandez, Pastors Johnny and Ruth Ortiz, and Pastors Josue and Benita Holguin have been a great godsend to us and are a huge blessing to have in our lives and ministry.

Second to last, I wholeheartedly thank God for the additional and great spiritual leadership covering Mildred and I are blessed to have, as two credentialed ministers of the North Texas District Council of the Assemblies of God. District Superintendent Dr. Gaylan Claunch, Assistant Superintendent Pastor Kermit Bell, and Secretary-Treasurer Pastor Gregg Headley are an exemplary executive leadership team in God's kingdom. Additionally, Senior Pastors Jim and Becky Hennesy of Trinity Church, in Cedar Hill, Texas, are one of the greatest pastoral couples Mildred and I have ever met. We are blessed to have them in our lives as well.

Lastly, to you, the reader, thank you for opening this book. I believe and pray its Bible-based, Christ-centered, and Spirit-filled message will greatly bless you, in the same way God used it to bless me. Thank you in advance for sharing it with others.

ENDORSEMENTS

Peter De Jesús is a man whose heart beats for revival in America. There are signs all around that God is sending another Great Awakening to the nations. In his new book, "Revival Now," Peter powerfully presents God's deep work throughout his life, creating in him a pursuit of God's presence and glory. Peter is experiencing an anointing to both preach and write a Biblical message on revival with historical insights that generate expectation and faith for a fresh outpouring of the Holy Spirit. Every so often, you meet a man who has been marked by God, and in his wrestling for revival, has been wounded and healed, but now walks with a limp like Jacob. Peter De Jesús is that man.

– Rev. Dennis Rivera
Director, Hispanic Relations of the Assemblies of God
A/G National Leadership and Resource Center,
Springfield, Missouri

"Revival Now" is a passionate cry of the Holy Spirit for God to Revive his work in the midst of a troubled world! Peter De Jesús has been anointed by the Holy Spirit to call for a fresh outpouring of Pentecostal power in signs, wonders, and miracles as believers of the first century experienced it. "Revival Now" flows out of the author's journey of faith and discovery of the authority of God's Word as the foundation for a fresh awakening to God's mission to reach the lost. The very title, "Revive Now," expresses the present urgency to apply the truths and principles Peter De Jesús has articulated so clearly!

– Dr. Gaylan Claunch
Superintendent, North Texas District Council A/G
Maypearl, Texas

In his book, "Revival Now," Peter De Jesús takes a bold step in sharing his personal journey of experiencing and overcoming fear, anxiety, and depression, among other obstacles, the devil tried to use to neutralize his life and ministry. The resulting personal breakthrough and revival has had a lasting impact among a new generation of believers. When you pick up this book it is more than just a good read. It is a spiritual journey of finding victory through the faithfulness of Jesus Christ and His church. May you too experience your breakthrough and personal revival.

– Pastor Kermit Bell
Assistant Superintendent, North Texas District Council A/G
Maypearl, Texas

"Revival Now" will stir the soul of every person that is believing and praying for the next Great Awakening in America. Peter De Jesús is a modern-day revivalist that has a passion for a fresh move of God in our churches and our nation. His personal revival led him back to the spiritual disciplines and Scriptural foundations that are needed for us to have a national revival. I encourage you to read his book with a heart that is open for a fresh outpouring of the Holy Spirit upon your life and a fresh impartation of His power through you to the lives of others.

– Pastor Gregg Headley
Secretary-Treasurer, North Texas District Council A/G
Maypearl, Texas

Nothing matters as much to America now, and the world, as a transformative activity of God which unveils His love and power. Peter De Jesús presents an inspiring and practical vision which stimulates hope and expectancy. This manual for a "last day" revival seems strategic to God's intention. A must read for hungry hearts!

– Rev. Jim Hennesy
Senior Pastor, Trinity Church
Cedar Hill, Texas

Throughout history, God has sent powerful revivals that have transformed the world. The last one was back in 1906. I wholeheartedly agree with Peter De Jesús that the Holy Spirit is preparing the world for revival, and that "History is in the making for the next Great Awakening." "Revival

Now" is about to be released worldwide. I praise God for using Peter to write this powerful book to prepare His church and the world for Revival Now. Get ready, Church, global revival is about to explode!

– Dr. Sergio Navarrete
Superintendent, Southern Pacific District A/G
Vice President, Global Hispanic Fraternity A/G
La Puente, California

I have known Rev. Peter De Jesús for over 20 years, as he served in different positions within the Youth Ministries Department in our district, having held the highest position within the department as its District Youth Director from 2000-2001. It is a great honor for me to endorse this book in such a time as this, when we are living in an unprecedented time of a pandemic crisis. It is divine timing for this book to become available now. This book gives awareness of what depression is, what it can do to a person, and how that individual can be helped. It also emphasizes the importance of the Church getting ready for the greatest revival the world has experienced. Lastly, it expresses the great importance of spreading the gospel to every person, so that everyone gets to know who Jesus is, and so the Scripture is fulfilled that one day "every knee shall bow and every tongue shall confess that Jesus Christ is Lord."

– Rev. Manuel Álvarez
Superintendent, Spanish Eastern District A/G
Old Tappan, New Jersey

Peter De Jesús' book "Revival Now" is more than just a book. It is a download from heaven, a prophetic roadmap that is strategically setting the Church up for its greatest moment in history. Peter is a modern day "man of Issachar" who understands the times we are living in, and through his penned pages of "Revival Now," you will be challenged to usher in the next Great Awakening! "Revival Now" is more than a must read. It is a MUST LIVE!

– Rev. Eleazar Rodríguez, Jr.
Superintendent, Texas Louisiana Hispanic District A/G

Pastor, Vida City Church Houston
Houston, Texas

"Revival Now" will stir you and encourage you to pray, fast, and long for revival, not later, but now. Peter De Jesús has a mandate and challenges every believer to go beyond every goal and pursue much needed revival. I encourage you to read this book carefully and allow the Holy Spirit to direct and edify you.

– Rev. Amos Garza
Superintendent, South Central Hispanic District A/G
Fort Worth, Texas

"Revival Now" is a much-needed call to God's people to earnestly seek the face of God. Peter De Jesús takes us on an incredible journey, starting with his life experience that leads him to the writing of this book, onto the path of why we need to seek God to send revival once again. Peter shares the needed stages for and rudiments of revival, which will help us experience revival in our lives in the times we live in. It is a great read and will instill the desire to see revival in our lives and in those we love. This book is a great resource to help you take your church through a step by step teaching on how to see revival in your church family. The amount of Scripture used throughout the book will clearly substantiate Peter's points. You will be moved to seek revival now in your life and church, and to accept the challenge of joining the 40-day fast! Revival will come, now.

– Rev. Jesse Galindo
Superintendent, Central Pacific Ministry Network A/G
Sacramento, California

"Revival Now" is an overwhelming account of the hunger and heart of Peter De Jesús in search for closeness with God. Many events in our lives serve as opportunities to take a step closer to God. In his book, Peter reveals surprise encounters where he heard the inner voice of God and experienced divine encounters where an intentional sacrifice was made to be alone with God. Through reading this book, you will see a hungry heart in preparation to hear the soft, still voice of God. You will learn that in sickness, pain, and suffering, God is always present and working on your behalf. Your heart will be moved, as you read this humble story of one person on a journey to connect with God. I genuinely believe in reading this book, you will hear from God yourself. This is a great read and a great challenge.

– Rev. Gilbert Daniel Olivarez
Superintendent, Central District A/G
Denver, Colorado

When Jesus gave the instructions to His disciples to wait for the promise of the Father, He mentioned they would receive power from the Holy Spirit. The disciples were able to experience the power and move of the Spirit of God in the book of Acts. In this book, Peter De Jesús inspires us to long for the renewal and the reawakening of the Holy Spirit again in God's people. After Peter's personal struggles in life, which tried to hinder his calling, God, through His mercy, still fulfills His plan in Peter's life. Peter seeks for the moving of the Holy Spirit again. God sends the Acts revival again. May that be your desire and passion as you read this book.

– Rev. Ezequiel Pecina
Superintendent, West Texas and Plains District A/G
Pastor, Life Church
Abilene, Texas

The beginning of a revival starts when we see our need for revival. Then we begin to pray for revival, until we desire to live so close to God and see His kingdom come, that we will settle for nothing less. When God sends revival, He will send it to a nation and a world through His church. "Revival Now" by Peter Jesús will help us go through this process and become the Church God wants for this time in history. It will take revival for us to bring in the harvest and make disciples. This book could not have come at a better time.

– Rev. Emilio De La Cruz
Superintendent, Southwest District A/G

Phoenix, Arizona

"Revival Now" is a book that challenges us to seek God for a Great Awakening. As Peter Jesús writes in his book, "we must understand that God has revived other generations in times past, and He can mercifully do it again in our present times." This is a must-read book!

– Rev. Clemente Maldonado, Jr.
Superintendent, Midwest Latin American District A/G
Oak Brook, Illinois

"Revival Now," like its author, Peter De Jesús, is a passionate, straightforward, and thorough presentation of why it is now time that God's prophetic word be converted into God's present work.

– Rev. Hilario Garza
Superintendent, Northwest Hispanic District A/G
Kennewick, Washington

In "Revival Now," Peter De Jesús, shares the true experience we all need to have with the Holy Spirit. To speak on the theme of revival, one must have experienced a supernatural move of the Holy Spirit. Peter experienced this in his life and ministry. Today, more than ever, we must speak about the coming revival in preparation for the Church to have a new encounter with our Lord Jesus. For that reason, I recommend this book, which will not be just another book in your life. In fact, there will be a spiritual Great Awakening in the life of those who read it.

– Rev. Edson Dos Santos
Superintendent, Southern Latin District A/G
Greenville, South Carolina

Peter De Jesús' book, "Revival Now," is a clarion call from God for whosoever will and desperately desires to see revival. In every generation, God has always reserved a remnant that appears on the scene at a crucial time in human history. This generation is no different. This book is for all those who, not only desire to see revival, but also desire to be part of it. Revival was not just for then; revival is for NOW!

– Rev. Jaime Loya
Lead Pastor, Cross Church
San Benito, Texas

"Revival Now" has been written for a time like this. In times of uncertainty, confusion, and doubt we need clear words from clear voices to give us clear direction. My friend, Peter, has given us all a practical guide to experiencing a revival that could change the course of this nation. Read it carefully!

– Rev. Tim Ross
Lead Pastor, Embassy City
Irving, Texas

Any time we see crisis in the world, we know God is also doing something big. It spawns change, and anytime we see change, we see shifts. There are huge shifts going on right now in the world. "Revival Now," written by Peter De Jesús, is such a timely book for the whole world. If we ever needed revival, we need it now. This book definitely shifts stuff that has been blocking revival from occurring in our cities and beyond.

– Dr. Mathew Bismark
Founder, GForce Ministries
Chairman, African Youth Pastors and Leaders Council
Houston, Texas

Peter's heart burns for revival, and in this powerful book, he tells of his own personal journey. I believe it will encourage and ignite you with the fires of revival. Peter has been a great encouragement to our ministry and has always supported our mission of revival around the world. "Revival Now" will be a blessing to your life, and I pray it will start a fire in your heart that never goes out!

– Rev. Josh Radford
Evangelist, Revival Life Ministries

Deland, Florida

For over forty years, my father, Senior Evangelist Carlos Annacondia, and his ministry team, have been experiencing a continual revival in Argentina and South America. We strongly believe that in these times, our Lord Jesus is looking into the hearts of mankind in order to reveal Himself and release revival into lives, families, and nations. Therefore, I fervently encourage believers to let "Revival Now," written by Peter De Jesús, be an inspiration that will encourage and challenge you to experience and live a life of continual revival. This book will bless you, as it awakens your heart, spirit, hunger, and desire for a mighty move of God.

– Rev. Elias Annacondia
Evangelist, International Message of Salvation
Houston, Texas

Peter's contagious passion for revival is evident, as he writes to compel his audience to seek the face of God wholeheartedly. Combined with his personal testimony of revival and encouraging teachings on the rudiments for a biblical awakening, this book is sure to guide its readers towards spiritual intimacy with the Lord. Peter's refreshing message of hope and hunger for a move of God, both "recruits and releases the Church for revival now." You will be blessed and encouraged, as you read and glean from each page with inspired truth for every believer in every season of life.

– Rev. Michael Fernández
Next Gen Director, Cornerstone Church, San Antonio, Texas

Throughout the years, Peter De Jesús has modeled, for me and so many others, what a life of Godly intimacy looks like. Peter's heart cry for revival in our generation is more than emotionalism. By God's grace, Peter has experienced God's glory, even during challenging times. I am confident that Peter's story and message will encourage you and ignite a fresh passion in you to experience your personal revival now.

– Rev. Luis "Nino" González

Campus Pastor, Cornerstone Central, Cornerstone Church
San Antonio, Texas

Over a decade ago, I began my venture into full time ministry under the leadership and guidance of Peter De Jesús. The knowledge, wisdom, and direction I gained while serving as a member of his staff are invaluable and are some of my fondest memories in ministry. Today, I am honored to call him a mentor and a friend. As someone who experienced a personal revival, while walking alongside him, I can tell you that Peter is the real deal! A passion for Holy Spirit revival stirs deeply inside him, and I believe God has called Peter for such a time as this to inform, inspire, and challenge the Body of Christ with the words written in "Revival Now!"

– Bryan Apodaca
Worship Leader, Cornerstone Central, Cornerstone Church
San Antonio, Texas

Peter's life embodies discipline, endurance, and revival. He has endured great trials and has come forth as a powerhouse to the glory of God. Since I have the privilege of working with him on a weekly basis, believe me when I say, he is a great inspiration to all. This book will both inspire and challenge you to reach for all God has for you and your ministry. In these challenging times, this book comes as a breath of fresh air. What we need today, more than ever, is "Revival Now."

– Rev. Daniel González
Spanish Pastor, Cornerstone Iglesia, Cornerstone Church
San Antonio, Texas

Peter has been a pillar of love, guidance, encouragement, and Kingdom power for my family. His contagious faith and reverence for Jesus has been an integral part of my life and faith journey. I have seen first-hand many of the seasons and accounts Peter shares in this book. I am not only a witness of his revival season, but a grateful byproduct of it as well. I highly encourage you to read "Revival Now" and stir up your faith for God to bring forth revival into your life.

– Rev. Andrew Cabasa
Next Gen Ministry Support Associate, Cornerstone Church
San Antonio, Texas

I witnessed firsthand the personal revival of Peter De Jesús, and his latest book "Revival Now" will encourage anyone who is seeking a move of God in their life. Peter takes readers through a fascinating study of revival and invites them to experience it for themselves. This book not only sparks revival fire, but it also provides the tools to personally experience a Great Awakening.

– Rev. Brett Owen
Creative Director, Epic Entertainment
Former Children's Pastor, Cornerstone Church
and Cornerstone Christian Schools
San Antonio, Texas

"Revival Now" conveys a message of expectancy for revival and the next Great Awakening. Peter De Jesús is transparent and clear with the basic principles for a personal and corporate revival. His book will motivate you to experience God in a more intimate way so that you can experience revival.

– Rev. Johnny Ortiz
Pastor, Catalyst Church
Regional Youth Director, Church of God South Central Region
San Antonio, Texas

Peter De Jesús is an anointed, gifted minister with a unique multi-cultural impact. His book, "Revival Now," lays a clear outline for revival, while intertwining relevant, practical principles with powerful testimonies. You will be blessed, and your spirit refreshed, as you read this call to revival!

– Rev. Josue Holguin
Spanish Pastor, Life Church
San Antonio, Texas

CONTENTS

FOREWORD

We are living in days when intercessors are storming the heavens. Our nation needs a powerful outpouring of the Holy Spirit. Lord, send us Revival!

"Revival Now" is a timely book. The Church needs to be challenged. We alone hold the answer to our nation's problems. The Lord gave us the prescription for our nation's pain in 2 Chronicles 7:14.

> *[14] If My people who are called by My name will humble themselves, and pray and seek my face, and turn from their wicked ways, then I will hear from heaven, and will forgive their sin and heal their land.*
>
> *2 Chronicles 7:14 NKJV*

I have prayed for revival for 62 years. During that journey, the Lord has shown me that a time would come when, in His mercy, He would pour out His Spirit. Whilst we wait, He has been preparing for that day. His preparation is people. In prayer, I have called out to the Lord to raise up an army of people carrying the fire of revival in their hearts. Graciously, He has been bringing individuals to life with a hunger for the heart of God to be revealed upon the earth. An Evan Roberts or a Charles Finney do not just happen. God works His special work in and through them, fitting them for use in that glorious day when He will come. I believe that something of that work has taken place in Peter De Jesús.

Peter was invited to the City Reachers Conference in February 2010, where Guillermo Maldonado was ministering. I considered Peter to be a young man being trained by the Lord to carry revival fire. So it was significant that Guillermo called Peter up to pray for him. Peter is one of those, marked for our day, who the Lord is calling to address a backslidden generation. We need an army of powerfully anointed revivalists to arise, such as was present in the ministry of Evan Roberts in the Welsh Revival. There is a huge harvest of souls to be reaped, and only the power of the Holy Spirit will meet the need.

I recommend "Revival Now" for all who are hungry for more, all who cry out for revival, all who are prepared to count the cost and follow Jesus through the Cross, all the way to Pentecost. Read "Revival Now" prayerfully and ask the Lord, "What should I do to spread revival fire?"

Eileen Vincent
Founder and President
Outpouring Ministries and City Reachers
San Antonio, Texas

FOREWORD

"Revival Now" gives us a window into the heart of all those who hunger to see revival. God uses His intercessors to pave the way for the work He intends to do. When He sought to protect the UK from air bombing during WWII, He raised up intercession through Rees Howells and his Swansea Bible School. When He was about to release tremendous healings and salvations in Argentina, He began in a powerful prayer meeting there, telling a young girl to pound on the table. When she did, the Holy Spirit filled the room and from there, a tremendous revival broke out! As the great revivalist John Wesley declared, "God does nothing except in response to prayer."

Revival history, the revelation of Jesus, and the Kingdom of God, has informed all of our praying. We pray the word of God, what it says and more importantly what it means, for it truly reflects the heart and purposes of God. It reflects all that He is looking for in individual lives, cities, states, and nations. He wants to revive those whose spirit is dead and dying and restore humanity to a living relationship with Himself. He desires that we all experience a personal revival and be used of Him to share that experience with the world around us.

That same passion filled our prayer meetings where on one Friday night in March 2010 Peter De Jesús joined us. It was there that Peter first declared in prayer at the open microphone, "Revival Now!" I remember the moment distinctly. That cry reverberated through the meeting. It was as a result of those times of prayer that we decided to call together citywide youth pastors with their youth groups to enter this realm of the spirit of prayer, worship, and faith. Those were powerful times of prayer, the power of which continues to impact hearts and lives today.

God uses revived people to bring revival. We pray for you, as you read this book, that its message brings you to a place of seeking personal revival so that you can be used of God to stir it wherever He appoints you. May there be a collective cry for Revival NOW!

Natalie Hardy
Executive Director
Outpouring Ministries and City Reachers
San Antonio, Texas

INTRODUCTION
MY PERSONAL REVIVAL STORY

Thank you for reading this book. "Revival Now: History is in the Making for the Next Great Awakening" is more than just an intriguing book title about a great global divine intervention gravely needed in our lifetime. Only by God's grace, and for His glory, is it also about a personal testimony I experienced, during a specific season in my life. Yet, before I share with you a vulnerable summary of my personal revival story, from August 2008 through May 2013, I believe it is of utmost importance for me to mention the time during which I am now writing this book.

The year is 2020. The season is Spring, from its start to its end. Thus far in this year, the world has been plagued by the unprecedented global pandemic of COVID-19, also known as the novel coronavirus. Over 8.7 million people worldwide have already contracted this plague and over 464,000 people have died, as a result. Consequently, the economy around the world has been devastated, including that of the United States of America, where I live. As of June 20th, over 40 million people in America have been unemployed this year and news outlets have been fearfully forecasting the possibility of the next Great

1

Depression occurring in our nation, as it first did from 1929 to 1939. Additionally, due to the recent grave injustice of multiple racial homicides committed, by civilians and police officers alike, against Black and White American civilians and police officers, racial tensions have increasingly escalated to an all-time high in recent years. The results have been unrelenting protests, riots, looting, and violence across our nation like never seen before in my lifetime. Hence, the gravity of our current times is grossly contributing to a season of great depression in many ways and on multiple levels in our society.

Yet, as I write this book, in my home in Lancaster, Texas, where I live in a predominantly Black community, as a Christian who happens to be a white-complected Puerto Rican, I sense a Bible-based, Christ-centered, Spirit-led, and faith-filled expectation that the next Great Awakening could actually occur in our nation over the course of the next decade. That is, of course, if our multiethnic nation and the multicolored Body of Jesus Christ are to first return to our One God and seek first His kingdom, just as 2 Chronicles 7:13-14 and Matthew 6:33-34 call us to do so.

> [13] *When I shut up heaven and there is no rain, or command the locusts to devour the land, or send pestilence among My people,* [14] *if My people who are called by My name will humble themselves, and pray and seek My face, and turn from their wicked ways, then I will hear from heaven, and will forgive their sin and heal their land.*
>
> *2 Chronicles 7:13-14 NKJV*

> [33] *But seek first the kingdom of God and His righteousness, and all these things shall be added to you.* [34] *Therefore do not worry about tomorrow, for tomorrow will worry about its own things. Sufficient for the day is its own trouble.*
>
> *Matthew 6:33-34 NKJV*

According to these two passages of scripture, if and when we seek God as we should and make Him and His kingdom our first priority, then the result will be our merciful God greatly responding to our biblically prescribed return to Him. Furthermore, our graceful God will add everything to us we are desperately in need of in this time, starting with revival now, and continue with His great forgiveness, healing, health, wealth, and racial reconciliation for His people of all ethnicities. Therefore, I believe we can have another Great Awakening, instead of another Great Depression. In fact, I dare to say that when the next Great Awakening occurs in the near future, it will be closely followed by a greater commitment to Christ's Great Commission registered in Matthew 28, so the greatest harvest of souls in our nation, and around the world, can be brought into God's great kingdom in the end times we are presently living in as mentioned in Luke 21.

[18] And Jesus came and spoke to them, saying, "All authority has been given to Me in heaven and on earth. [19] Go therefore and make disciples of all the nations, baptizing them in the name of the Father and of the Son and of the Holy Spirit, [20] teaching them to observe all things that I have commanded you; and lo, I am with you always, even to the end of the age." Amen.

Matthew 28:18-20 NKJV

[10] Then He said to them, "Nation will rise against nation, and kingdom against kingdom. [11] And there will be great earthquakes in various places, and famines and pestilences; and there will be fearful sights and great signs from heaven. [12] But before all these things, they will lay their hands on you and persecute you, delivering you up to the synagogues and prisons. You will be brought before kings and rulers for My name's sake. [13] But it will turn out for you as an occasion for testimony."

Luke 21:10-13 NKJV

In fact, I believe all of this, including the great signs from heaven such as the four blood moon (lunar eclipses) of this year occurring in January, June, July, and November[1], will serve as a prophetic precursor to the great and awesome day of the Lord, according to Joel 2 and Acts 2.

> [30] *And I will show wonders in the heavens and in the earth:*
> *Blood and fire and pillars of smoke.*
> [31] *The sun shall be turned into darkness,*
> *And the moon into blood,*
> *Before the coming of the great and awesome day of the*
> *LORD.*
> [32] *And it shall come to pass*
> *That whoever calls on the name of the LORD*
> *Shall be saved.*
>
> *Joel 2:30-32a NKJV*

> [19] *I will show wonders in heaven above*
> *And signs in the earth beneath:*
> *Blood and fire and vapor of smoke.*
> [20] *The sun shall be turned into darkness,*
> *And the moon into blood,*
> *Before the coming of the great and awesome day of the*
> *LORD.*
> [21] *And it shall come to pass*
> *That whoever calls on the name of the LORD*
> *Shall be saved.'*
>
> *Acts 2:19-21 NKJV*

Yet, before I proceed with the thought of the next Great Awakening for a renewed Great Commission in preparation for the greatest harvest of souls occurring over the next decade prior to the rapture of the Church and the Great Tribulation on earth, I sense the need to reflect on the last decade. The reason for this notion is to revisit the historic personal revival I experienced during that time, and to connect it to the times in which we are now living. In doing so, I must state, that I believe what I am about to share with you is both a timeless, and timely, message for the multiethnic Body of Jesus Christ in our nation and around the world. In fact, I especially believe this for ministers and leaders who, like me, have either, in the past, dealt with, or are presently dealing with, mental health challenges and the need to spiritually experience a personal revival that will result in a corporate spiritual awakening. For then, and only then, would we have the power in Christ Jesus to change the course of history in our very own lives, families, communities, states, nation, and beyond.

Therefore, please allow me to proceed by transparently sharing with you how what began in June of 2008 as a "dream come true" ministry opportunity, eventually became a "living nightmare" in my personal life and ministry, until God mercifully and faithfully revived me. What was the "dream come true" ministry opportunity all about? On Sunday, May 25, 2008, while living in San Antonio, Texas, I had the great honor of personally meeting the world-renowned Founding Senior Pastor, Dr. John Hagee, and his son, Lead Pastor, Matthew Hagee, of Cornerstone Church, which has over 20,000 members in its non-denominational and multiethnic congregation. This great honor was granted to me by my dear brother and friend, Evangelist Dr. Chris Hill, who ministered powerfully at Cornerstone Church that night. After enjoying the service and a subsequent dinner with Pastor Matthew Hagee, Dr. Hill, and a few others, I was flattered to have been invited to meet with Pastor Matthew ten days later, on Wednesday, June 4th. On that day, both Pastor Matthew and Pastor Hagee graciously invited me to join their pastoral staff. The role I would eventually begin serving in, as of Monday, August 25th, would be that of their Cornerstone Church High School Youth Pastor and their Cornerstone Christian Schools' Secondary School Campus Pastor.

Of course, I was blown away by this great opportunity. In fact, this invitation held special significance for me personally. The reason

5

being that seventeen years prior to that time, when I was just 16 years of age, there were three internationally well-known ministers, whose radio and television ministries had greatly impacted my life. More so to the point that, at that time, I had asked the Lord to please give me a measure of His anointing that was on their lives. Interestingly enough, those three ministers were Pastor John Hagee, Pastor John Osteen, and Pastor Benny Hinn.

Therefore, for me to be asked by one of them, 17 years later, at age 33, to join his pastoral staff was a surreal experience, to say the least. As a result, I felt like I was walking in heavenly clouds while looking forward to bringing heaven down upon a generation of young people at Cornerstone Church, Cornerstone Christian Schools, and the city of San Antonio. Now as much as I would love to say that was exactly what began to happen right away, regretfully and with all transparency, I cannot.

Unfortunately, the honest-to-God truth is that within weeks of starting my role at Cornerstone, I began to experience a gradual downward spiral of a miserable 18-month season of depression. This season began and progressed with personal thoughts and feelings of inadequacy, fear, doubt, stress, anxiety, panic attacks, confusion, and disbelief in my very own ministerial calling and gifting. This was primarily due to my very own faults, in addition to Satan's attack against my life, and God's sovereign plan for me.

Needless to say, it is worth noting that this very difficult season I experienced does not reflect negatively in any way, shape, or form on the faithful, compassionate, wise, powerful, and anointed leadership of Pastor Hagee, Pastor Mathew, and the wonderful pastoral staff at Cornerstone Church, for whom I am forever grateful. Yet with regards to continuing my description of the most difficult season I have ever experienced to this day, I believe it would be helpful for me to share more about what I endured. In fact, I will never forget the first time in my life that I experienced a panic attack.

It occurred on a Monday night to a Tuesday morning, November 10-11th, before ministering at a Cornerstone Christian Schools

6

Secondary Campus Chapel service. The panic attack was unlike anything I had ever experienced in my prior eleven years of ministry in various roles including those of an Assemblies of God district youth director, associate pastor, worship pastor, co-pastor, campus pastor, and adjunct bible institute professor. Yet, this panic attack was just the beginning, as things became even worse for me.

By January of 2009, and thereafter, I also began to experience a growing loss of appetite, an increasing inability to sleep well, and feeling physiological strange sensations and numbness in different parts of my body, such as my limbs, neck, and head. I later found out, from my family doctor, that what I was experiencing was actually associated with extremely high levels of stress. I also discovered, through my personal research about depression, that everything I had experienced up to this point was related to clinical depression. All the while, I attempted to do the best I could to be a successful High School Youth Pastor and Secondary School Campus Pastor, at one of the greatest mega-churches and private Christian schools on planet earth. However, I must admit that I felt like a failure.

Just when I thought this season could not get any more difficult, in January and February of 2009, I experienced two unsuccessful visits to my family doctor, in my attempt to begin taking medication for depression. The reason why I say my doctor visits were unsuccessful was because both the name-brand and generic medications my doctor prescribed for me were not covered by my health insurance and they were far too expensive for me to afford. Consequently, I had to find another way to cope with the season of depression I was experiencing. Unfortunately, my condition did not get any better. In fact, it got so bad that one night in April of 2009, around 1:00 a.m., I woke up restlessly, due to the numbness I was experiencing in one of my arms and shoulders. I actually thought I was possibly having a heart attack. After immediately waking up my wife, Mildred, having her pray for me, and assessing with her what I was experiencing, I was able to get back to sleep and rest a bit. Unfortunately, what I was going through became so

7

bad that I began to feel like the prophet Elijah, in 1 Kings 19:4, who at a particular point in his life, and time in ministry, wanted to die.

> *4 But he himself went a day's journey into the wilderness, and came and sat down under a broom tree. And he prayed that he might die, and said, "It is enough! Now, LORD, take my life, for I am no better than my fathers!"*
>
> *1 Kings 19:4 NKJV*

Although I was not battling suicidal thoughts or tendencies, I did begin to honestly think that it would be best for me if God were to just let me go to sleep and die, allowing me to wake up on the other side of eternity, only by His grace and mercy. Consequently, throughout this time, I obtained approximately a half million dollars in life insurance through multiple life insurance policies. My thought was that if I did die in my sleep, at least Mildred, and our three children, would be taken care of financially for several years. It was that bad. Consequently, I eventually decided I would ask Pastor Matthew if we could set up one of our periodic one-on-one meetings for Monday, May 11, 2009. My original plan for the meeting was for me to humbly hand him my letter of resignation. The meeting was set for that date, but two days before, on Saturday, May 9th, my resignation plan was divinely interrupted by God's powerful intervention through my wife. During what felt like a mental meltdown I experienced that Saturday, Mildred began to pray over me, speak God's word to me, and remind me that God was not done with me yet. She also reminded me that God had not brought me this far so I could quit on Him. We had an immensely powerful moment in God's glorious presence, and I was so blessed to have such a godly wife, full of faith in God's word, and committed to prayer.

Once I realized that I was not going to resign, I decided to do the next best thing, which was to be completely integral and transparent with Pastor Matthew and tell him everything I had been experiencing for the prior eight months. Although I did this with fear and trembling, I thank God for the way Pastor Matthew gracefully responded to me. He loved

8

me. He encouraged me. He supported me. He made it crystal clear that he believed in me and my calling from the Lord. After he shared with Pastor Hagee some of what I had shared with him, Pastor Hagee, soon thereafter, also made it noticeably clear to me that he was fighting the good fight of faith together with me in prayer. To have them both in my corner, in addition to Mildred, our three children, and my parents, meant so much to me.

As a result, I fully recognized that it was time for me to spiritually fight the good fight of faith, more than ever before. More importantly, I realized I needed to draw closer to the Lord and seek Him for more of His supernatural help. Therefore, in the latter part of the Spring through the Summer of 2009, I attended several of our Cornerstone Church Ministry of Reconciliation Encounter Weekends, led by Pastor Philip Fortenberry. I also attended a couple of professional counseling sessions with a local Christian licensed counselor, who Pastor Matthew had wisely recommended to me. The combination of these two types of essential ministry was powerful and effective, as the Lord utilized them to minister to me in spiritual healing, deliverance, and biblically based counseling and life-coaching. In fact, and as strange as it might sound, when I met with the Christian licensed counselor and asked him to still write me a prescription for depression medication, he let me know that based on his professional assessment and spiritual discernment, I did not need a medical prescription. Instead, he took hold of his office notepad and began to write something on it. When he finished writing, he tore off the top sheet and handed it to me. Although part of me still expected to see a medical prescription written on it, to my surprise what I read was "Isaiah 60:1-2."

> *¹ Arise, shine; For your light has come! And the glory of the LORD is risen upon you. ² For behold, the darkness shall cover the earth, And deep darkness the people; But the LORD will arise over you, And His glory will be seen upon you.*
>
> *Isaiah 60:1-2 NKJV*

Now I must admit, when I saw "Isaiah 60:1-2" written on that sheet of paper, instead of a medical prescription, it completely caught me off guard, especially coming from a professional licensed counselor. Yet, God knew what I needed to see and hear at that precise moment in time. In fact, God is so sovereign He not only used the pastoral staff from Cornerstone Church, together with my wife and parents to speak biblically based words of counsel to me, but He also used the Christian licensed counselor to remind me of God's word over my life. By August of 2009, I came to the full realization I desperately needed to return to the spiritual disciplines and fundamental basics of my relationship with God. So, I did. Soon afterward, in September of that year, I profoundly discovered my deep need and growing desire to experience a personal revival. Thus, I began to pursue the Lord, much more than I had done so in the prior year. As I did so, I then began to sense God calling me, towards the end of 2009, to prepare to go on a 40-day fast in 2010.

As the new year rolled around, I continued to seek the Lord even more. In fact, the human sense of obligation to seek the Lord as a minister was gloriously replaced by a spiritual obsession to seek the Lord as a lover of His presence. Soon thereafter, during a dinner with my extended family in February of 2010, my cousin, Perry Santana, who at the time was the worship pastor at Abundant Life Church of God (ALCOG) in San Antonio, led by Pastor Eliezer Bonilla, told me about a City Reacher's Conference that was going to be hosted at ALCOG on the third week of February. This conference was organized by the great and late Apostle Alan Vincent, his precious wife Eileen Vincent, and their Executive Director, Natalie Hardy, of Outpouring Ministries and City Reachers based in San Antonio. At the same family dinner, one of my other cousins, Pastor Ray Maldonado of New Life Ministries of San Antonio, who had been my pastor during my high school years, accepted the invitation to join me in attending the conference. One of the main reasons we decided to do so was because its main conference speaker was going to be Apostle Guillermo Maldonado of King Jesus Ministry in Miami, Florida.

That night, on Tuesday, February 16th, before the service began, my cousin Perry introduced Pastor Ray and me to Apostle Alan and Eileen Vincent, and during the service we received a powerful message from Apostle Maldonado on the biblical theme of living with "Supernatural Faith" in King Jesus. We were blessed to have been able to sit on the front row next to the Vincent's and other ministers. Following the message, Apostle Maldonado made an altar call, and I made sure to respond to it as quickly as possible. Of approximately 900 people in the service, about 25 of us were called by Apostle Maldonado to come up to the platform to receive prayer from him. When the moment came for him to pray for me, all the Lord had him do, from about six feet away from me, was declare the word "peace" over my life. The next thing I knew was that I was laid out on the platform, under the supernatural power of God. It was truly a supernatural moment God used to continue to greatly minister to me.

About a week later, God was strongly impressing upon me to get ready to start a 40-day fast. As I prayed about it, I asked Him to at least allow me to start the fast after a birthday dinner for my son, David Samuel, on Sunday, February 28th. I sensed the Lord mercifully accept my request and I planned to fast from the late night of February 28th through Friday, April 9th. However, I had no idea April 9th was profoundly significant, as it pertains to revival history. It was not until three years later in 2013, that Lou Engle, Founder of The Call, who had accepted my invitation for him to minister at Cornerstone Church's young adult ministry, told me about April 9th being the anniversary of the 1906 Azusa Street Revival in Los Angeles, California. I had no idea of the great significance of April 9th.

Now as a prelude to the start of my fast on the night of February 28th, I accepted the invitation from my dear brother and friend Brett Owen, Children's Pastor of Cornerstone Church, to attend a special Wednesday night service, on February 24th, at his father's home church, Oasis Church in San Antonio, Texas, led by Pastor Dennis Goldsworthy-Davis. That night, the guest minister was Rev. Dutch Sheets, of Dutch Sheets Ministries in Leesville, South Carolina. He preached a prophetic and profound message based on Genesis 26:18 regarding "re-digging the wells of revival" so that an even greater kingdom revival would spring forth.

> [18] *And Isaac dug again the wells of water which they had dug in the days of Abraham his father, for the Philistines had stopped them up after the death of Abraham. He called them by the names which his father had called them.*
>
> *Genesis 26:18 NKJV*

It was such a powerful message, needless to say. In fact, I sensed God use that message to have me focus on believing Him to release another kingdom revival in San Antonio. Soon afterwards, I began my fast on the late night of February 28th, and I was determined to experience revival in my life, family, and ministry. Then on the night of Tuesday, March 9, 2010, Pastor Matthew led one of our monthly Joshua's Generation Prayer Meetings at Cornerstone Church. During this prayer meeting, he asked for the pastors of the children, youth, young adults, and young married couples ministries to come to the front to be anointed with oil and be prayed for by him. As a result, when the time came for Pastor Matthew to anoint me and pray for me, the Lord led him to specifically focus on praying for an anointing to unite the Body of Christ. I later found out why this anointing was extremely important for revival in my life, ministry, and the city of San Antonio, especially as it pertained to the younger generation.

By this time, the undercurrent of God's wave of revival was well underway in me. Consequently, things were beginning to heavenly shift from the past season of depression into a present season of revival. Shortly thereafter, I accepted an invitation I had received to attend one of the weekly Friday night City Reachers' Prayer Meetings led by Eileen Vincent and Natalie Hardy, who I met the month before at their conference. These prayer meetings, which were attended by Christians of all ethnicities from various churches throughout San Antonio, began approximately at 10:00 p.m. and would go until at least midnight or later.

I must say these meetings were such a blessing to all who attended them, especially to me who received personal prayer from Eileen and Natalie during and beyond these prayer meetings.

In fact, on a particular and momentous occasion during one of their Friday night prayer meetings in March 2010, during which they allowed multiple ministers to lead everyone in prayer, they graced me with the same opportunity. As I prayed about "now being the time for revival," I mentioned in my prayer the phrase "revival now." Of course, I had no earthly idea of what would come forth from that prayer. All I knew was that there was a special anointing on that declaration of prayer for revival now. All the while, I was full swing into my 40-day fast, which was a combination of a 21-day Daniel fast (eating only fruit, vegetables, grains, and liquids), a 7-day liquid fast, a 3-day Esther fast (having no food nor drinks), and a 9-day Daniel fast, in that order.

When I ended my fast on Friday, April 9th, something had completely shifted in my life. The 18-month season of depression had ended, and a new and greater season of revival had begun. Now I was closer, than ever before, to the Lord. I had more divine confidence from the Lord. I began to see God restore all the spiritual, emotional, physical, relational, and ministerial aspects of my life. But now they were restored with so much more.

Yet, God was not done with me yet. In fact, to my surprise, ten days after my 40-day fast, I sensed the Lord internally speak to me and tell me, "Give me another 40 days." Little did I know, in principle, God was doing something similar in my life He had done in the life of Moses with regards to two back to back 40-day fasts, as noted in Deuteronomy 9:18 which says:

> [18] *And I fell down before the LORD, as at the first, forty days and forty nights; I neither ate bread nor drank water, because of all your sin which you committed in doing wickedly in the sight of the LORD, to provoke Him to anger.*
> *Deuteronomy 9:18 NKJV*

Yet truth be told, since I was now revived and restored across the board, I honestly and humanly did not like the fact that God was asking me for more. However, because I was so grateful to Him who was more than faithful to me, I said "yes" to 40 more days from Monday, April 19th through Friday, May 28th. However, what was distinct about this second 40-day fast was that the Lord spoke to my heart and told me that I did not have to fast food during this fast. As strange as that sounds, instead, I sensed the Lord asking me to fast two hours of sleep each night from 11:00 p.m. to 1:00 a.m. When I had asked Him why He wanted me to pray during those hours, He reminded me that He is our Alpha and Omega, and He let me know that He wanted me to give Him the alpha and omega hours of a 24-hour period. Interestingly enough, I sensed the Lord was fine with me taking evening naps after dinner each night, as long as I would wake up with enough time to start praying at 11:00 p.m. What was also distinct about this second 40-day fast was that the Lord spoke to my spirit and impressed upon me that He wanted me to specifically pray for unity in the Body of Christ, instead of praying solely for revival from Christ. He revealed to me that one of the most important, yet missing, ingredients for corporate revival in Christ's church, beyond a personal revival in an individual believer, is unity amongst all Christian believers.

Therefore, it was at this time that I understood a bit more as to why God had led Pastor Matthew on Tuesday night, March 9th, to pray for me and anoint me specifically with regards to unity in the multiethnic Body of Christ. With that understanding, I began to pray each night from 11:00 p.m. to 1:00 a.m., and specifically prayed for unity amongst Christians, churches, pastors, and leaders, especially for those leading young people as I was doing so at the time. Now just when things were going seemingly well in this second 40-day fast, something went severely wrong on the 25th day of the fast. Although I had set my alarm to wake up around 10:30 p.m. on Thursday night, May 13th, I overslept and woke up at 1:30 a.m. on Friday morning, May 14th. I had slept through my alarm, and my prayer time. When I realized what had happened, I felt so bad and condemned.

Then God, who is so merciful and faithful, spoke to my heart and reminded me of Romans 8:1 which says:

> *¹ There is therefore now no condemnation to those who are in Christ Jesus, who do not walk according to the flesh, but according to the Spirit.*
>
> *Romans 8:1 NKJV*

Therefore, I sensed the Lord tell me to shake off the condemnation and go pray. So, I did, and it was so wonderfully glorious. Little did I know my prayer time which started late at 1:30 a.m. would go for five hours straight until 6:30 a.m. on Friday, May 14th. What was so glorious about this prayer time was that it seemed to go by so fast, while God led me to pray through so many passages of scripture, from Genesis through Revelation. These Bible passages specifically had to do with unity, and the climactic highlight of these passages was none other than John 17. Why was this so important? Because it is in this chapter that Jesus Christ prays to our Heavenly Father for unity amongst His people on earth, as specifically noted in verses 20-23 which say:

> *²⁰ I do not pray for these alone, but also for those who will believe in Me through their word; ²¹ that they all may be one, as You, Father, are in Me, and I in You; that they also may be one in Us, that the world may believe that You sent Me. ²² And the glory which You gave Me I have given them, that they may be one just as We are one: ²³ I in them, and You in Me; that they may be made perfect in one, and that the world may know that You have sent Me, and have loved them as You have loved Me.*
>
> *John 17:20-23 NKJV*

What a glorious experience the Lord had graced me with that day. It was as if God mercifully enabled me to transcend time and space in that holy moment, so I could personally perceive the prayer for unity

Jesus Christ prayed on the day registered in John 17. The following night, I got back on track with praying from 11:00 p.m. to 1:00 a.m. and continued to do so until Friday, May 28th. By this time now, what started out a couple of months prior as a personal revival was now taking on a greater form and force for corporate revival. Unbeknownst to me, God had used Pastor Matthew's prayer and anointing me for unity to release a greater measure of revival in my life that included me, but was not exclusive to me. God revealed to me that He desired to have His revival come to me and flow through me to others around me.

To confirm this, the Lord placed in the hearts of my dear friends, Eileen and Natalie, to host another City Reachers Conference in June of 2010. This time, in addition to having services and sessions primarily for adults, this second conference would also include two youth services. When they prayerfully considered what the name and theme of the conference would be, they sensed the Lord tell them to call it "Revival NOW." That was, in part, based on what we had prayed for during one of their Friday Night Prayer Meetings I mentioned earlier. When they considered which ministers the Lord would have them invite to minister at this conference, in addition to the great men of God such as Chuck Pierce, Hector Torres, Johnny Ortiz, and other kingdom revival ministers, they also graced me with an invitation to minister in one of the youth services. That particular service occurred on Saturday, June 12, 2010. When I ministered by God's grace and for His glory, over 600 youth, young adults, and adults from at least 20 different ministries from all over the San Antonio Area attended that night. The message the Lord led me to share was on "Revival Now." It was a very abbreviated version of the message in this book. By the end of the night, hundreds of Hispanic, Black, and White American young people, from all over the city, were united in Christ Jesus and crying out for revival now. We all prayed for God to revive us personally, so He could also revive others corporately through His revival work in our lives. It was profoundly powerful. Yet, that was just the beginning.

I humbly believe that the personal revival God graced me with in 2010 contributed to a corporate revival and increase of unity in our youth ministries, city, and beyond. This then changed the course of our history and ushered in the beginning of a great awakening, especially among young people in our area and region. In fact, by God's divine design, and with Pastor Matthew's blessing, one of the results of the corporate revival of 2010 was the leadership formation, in November of that year, and the subsequent launching in January 2011, of a multiethnic relational fellowship for youth and young adult pastors and leaders. It was called "UNITE," and it still exists to this day led by Pastor Joel Garza. Together with twelve amazing Hispanic, Black, and White American youth pastors and young adult pastors in our city (Johnny Ortiz, Michael Fernandez, Michael Hernandez, Jarrell Flowers, David Robinson, Matthew Bell, Gavin Rogers, Oscar Guajardo, Sammy Lopez, David Mayorga, David Martin, and Tina Hidy-Marlin), I was honored to facilitate, various revival and unity efforts with all of our ministries and many more, including some regionally and nationally-known ministries. It is worth mentioning these great ministers were from great non-denominational churches and denominations such as the Assemblies of God, Church of God, San Antonio Baptist Association, United Methodist Church, Seventh Day Adventist, and the Catholic Church. Our Bible-based, Christ-centered, and Spirit-led unity in Christ and His kingdom, resulted in a great impact on the young people in our city and beyond. It was glorious to see multiethnic youth and young adults, from the inner-city to the outskirts of the city, unite under the Lordship of Jesus Christ.

Yet, just when I thought all of that was great enough, in April of 2011, God led Pastor Matthew, to have me serve as the Cornerstone Church College and Career Young Adult Pastor, in addition to still serving as the High School Youth Pastor. Together with our dear friends and great staff, comprised of Pastors Michael Fernandez, Nino Gonzalez, Bryan Apodaca, and approximately 70 multiethnic youth and young adult leaders, Mildred and I hosted citywide youth and young adult rallies for young people at Cornerstone Church and throughout our city. At these rallies, we were blessed to have guest ministers such as Lou Engle, Eddie James, Jeremy Johnson, Tim Ross, Robert Madu, Matthew Bismark, Josh Radford, Joe Oden, Frank Hechavarria, Gabby Mejia,

Mark Vega, Kari Jobe, Rick Pino, Jake Hamilton, and others come minister and help us keep the flames of revival growing. Those were indeed epic times for a new era of revival among the young people of our region.

Then in 2013, God gracefully blessed me with opportunity to write my first book titled "Now Is the Time: Accelerated Timing for Exponential Impact," for which Pastor Matthew wrote the foreword. Since then, that book has been distributed in English and in Spanish all over the nation, releasing a message of God's prophetic promise to His leaders and people, regarding the glory of the latter house being greater than the glory of the former house. Soon thereafter, in May of 2013, with Pastor Matthew's blessing, I transitioned from my dual pastoral staff role at Cornerstone Church to launch, together with Mildred, "De Jesus Ministries." To God's glory, since 2013 to this year, God has graced us with the privilege of ministering evangelistically, in English and Spanish, to over 150,000 people of all ages throughout our nation, Puerto Rico, Mexico, and Costa Rica, not including many more thousands we have ministered to through social media and other media platforms. For all this and so much more, I am profoundly thankful to our God of revival. The personal revival He graced me with in 2010, has contributed to the personal and corporate revival of thousands of people to this very day. All praise be to God!

Now it is your turn. Just as God graced me with a personal revival that resulted in a corporate revival, so I wholeheartedly believe God has a personal revival in store for you that will soon come to you, then flow through you, and thereafter reach countless of others around you. I dare to say this, not only based on my personal experience, but more importantly, based on what our Lord Jesus Christ prophesied and later fulfilled through the life of His disciple Peter, according to Luke 22:31-32 which says:

> [31] And the Lord said, "Simon, Simon! Indeed, Satan has
> asked for you, that he may sift you as wheat. [32] But I have

18

prayed for you, that your faith should not fail; and when
you have returned to Me, strengthen your brethren."
Luke 22:31-32 NKJV

Yes, just as Jesus Christ revived a fallen Peter, and then through his spiritually awakened life, Christ revived 120 other disciples who went with Peter to the upper room in preparation for the Day of Pentecost which resulted in 3,000 souls being saved as a first-fruit of many more thousands who were afterwards added to God's kingdom, so I believe Christ desires to do it again. This time, He can do it with you and through you, regardless of your gender, age, ethnicity, profession, social class, and any other human classification Satan and the secular world uses to attempt to divide us. In Christ, we can unite to advance God's kingdom.

So, get ready. History is in the making for the next great awakening, and it is time for revival now. If you believe this with me, then I invite you to open your mind, heart, soul, and spirit to this word of the Lord and to the Holy Spirit of our God, as you begin to read and experience "Revival Now."

CHAPTER 1
WHAT IS REVIVAL NOW?

What is revival now? That is the question I began to ask God, in the Spring of 2010, shortly after experiencing revival in my life and being informed, by my dear friends, Natalie Hardy and Eileen Vincent, that they sensed from the Lord to call their City Reachers Conference, that summer, "Revival NOW." This was due, in part, to the Lord leading me to pray for revival now during one of their City Reachers Friday Night Prayer Meetings in the month of March that same year. Little did I know, that in addition to all I mentioned in the introduction, ten years later, I would be writing the book about this powerful phrase and its prophetic message to the worldwide multiethnic Body of Christ during the COVID-19 global pandemic and heightened season of racial tension in our nation. To think that God could move in and through the life of someone like me, who battled with personal depression, in order to bring a message to the Church for corporate awakening is truly humbling and glorious. However, before I share with you the answer God gave me to my question of "What is revival now?," I believe it is important for me to share a bit about my background and introduction to revival.

Revival is a word I grew up hearing, due to being born on December 4, 1974 in Rochester, New York, where Evangelist Charles G. Finney led one of the great revivals of the Second Great Awakening, in 1830-31, resulting in approximately 100,000 salvations. It was in this city, marked by revival, where I was born into a Christian family of ten and raised in a Pentecostal home and church family led by my parents, Rev. Roberto and Carmen De Jesús. They, having been born in Puerto Rico and predominantly raised in the multiethnic melting pots of Manhattan and Bronx, NY, had experienced a radical Bible-based, Christ-centered, and Spirit-filled conversion, from a non-practicing state of Catholicism to a powerfully experienced lifestyle of Pentecostalism, during their mid-twenties. Many years later, by the time I was born as the seventh of their eight children, my parents had already experienced their own personal revival for several years. As a result, my father attended a Spanish Eastern District Assemblies of God Bible Institute in Manhattan, NY for one year, and a few years later, due to relocating to Rochester, graduated from the Assembly of Christian Churches Bible Institute, after three additional years of biblical studies. Thereafter, he received his ordination credentials from The Council of Missionary Churches of Christ, while serving in ministry at a local church. When I was two years of age, my father, together with my mother, began his first pastorate at the Pentecostal Mission bilingual church in the multicultural zip code area of 14621 in Rochester. I share all this to provide you with a general background of my parents, family, our faith, and my early upbringing, which was familiar with revival. I also share this purposefully in honor of my beloved parents and their great influence of revival on my life. Now more than ever, as they are in their elderly years of 75 and 74, I fully realize that their spiritual heritage and Pentecostal legacy is mine to continue and pass onto my children and future generations.

Fast forward eight years from when my parents began to pastor, and in 1984, the majority of my family relocated from Rochester to San Antonio, Texas. It was then, when I was age ten, that I accepted Jesus Christ as my personal Lord and Savior, during a Sunday night service in November, at El Salvador Assembly of God Church which was co-founded by the great late Rev. H.C. Ball and was, at the time, led by Pastor Ruben Serna. I am forever grateful for the ministry I received that night from the young adult students, of Latin American Bible Institute of the Assemblies of God, who were the guest ministers for that service. That night, I also received the baptism of the Holy Spirit and fire, with the evidence of speaking in heavenly tongues. Hence, slowly, but surely, I was becoming more familiar with revival.

Seven years later, at the age of 17, I accepted God's call on my life for ministry during the altar call of a worship concert I attended at the non-denominational Trinity Church in San Antonio. Interestingly enough, as mentioned in my introduction, this was the same year I asked the Lord to give me a portion of His anointing I had observed on the lives and ministries of Pastor John Hagee, Pastor John Osteen, and Pastor Benny Hinn. For me, these great men of God exemplified an anointing for revival. Watching and listening to their television and radio programs weekly, and sometimes even daily, had a great impact on my life. Additionally, during the same year, and the two years prior, I was deeply impacted by the life and ministry of my older cousin, Pastor Ray Maldonado of New Life Ministries of San Antonio. He was the first pastor to grace me with the privilege of serving in a congregation as a youth leader. Collectively, God used these four ministers and their ministries to powerfully influence my faith, even though, for the most part, it was from a distance, with the exception of my cousin, Pastor Ray. Collectively, they helped me to fan into flame the zeal for revival I increasingly desired, in preparation for future ministry.

At the age of 18, I pursued God's call on my life as a single young adult. Subsequently, in obedience to the Lord and with my parents' and pastor's blessing, together with the warm welcome of my eldest sister Debbie and my brother-in-law David Hernandez, I moved back to Rochester. It was there where I met my wife, Mildred, and where we became members at Light of the World Church Assembly of God led by Pastors Luis and Isabel Hernandez of the Spanish Eastern District of the Assemblies of God Northwest Section. Eventually, we moved onto Allentown and Easton, Pennsylvania, followed by moving to Staten

Island, NY, before later relocating to Dallas, TX, and then returning back to San Antonio in 2007.

However, thanks to our gracious God, at the age of 32, I did not return alone. Instead, I was very grateful to have returned with my lovely wife, who I married in 1996, and with our three precious children, who were born in 1997 through 2001. By that time, Mildred and I had already been credentialed ministers of the Assemblies of God since 1999, which was the same year in which we graduated from the Spanish Eastern District Assemblies of God Bible Institute in Staten Island, NY. By God's grace and for His glory, from 1997 through 2007, we served in many ministerial roles and had experienced our fair share of divinely granted successes in ministry resulting in glorious salvations, healings, deliverances, miracles, and more in the lives of thousands of people in New York, Pennsylvania, Texas, and beyond.

Increasingly, revival was becoming a living reality in our lives and ministry, and we were blessed to have been ministers with the Assemblies of God Spanish Eastern District, North Texas District, and South Texas District councils, from 1999 through 2007. During those years, I was greatly blessed to have served on the pastoral staff of three great churches, led by three great Pastors, who had been personally and ministerially very familiar with revival – Third Day Worship Center with Pastor Samuel Rodriguez, Jr. in Staten Island, NY, The Oaks Fellowship with Pastor Scott Wilson in Dallas, TX, and Valley Hi Assembly of God with Pastor Terry Richardson in San Antonio, TX. I am forever grateful for these great churches and great men of God who He utilized to greatly impact my life and ministry. Additionally, I am very thankful to Pastor Samuel Rodriguez, Jr., the late Superintendent Emeritus Dr. Adolfo Carrion, Superintendent Emeritus Rev. Rafael Reyes, and the Spanish Eastern District (SED) for allowing me to have served in the SED youth ministries from 1994 through 2001.

Moving along, in 2008, Mildred and I were graced to join the pastoral staff of Cornerstone Church, led by Pastor John Hagee and Pastor Matthew Hagee. The transformative personal and ministerial experiences I received, from 2008 through 2013, are noted in the prior introduction. After enduring a grave season of depression, for approximately 18 months, God mercifully gave me an even greater season of revival for the next 36 months and beyond. Through these two life-changing, polar-opposite, and back-to-back seasons, I learned that, although I had been born and raised in a revival-oriented home, had begun to experience revival in my childhood and youth, and had been introduced to and even participated in, revival ministries as a young adult, and thereafter, as a mature adult, I still needed to experience a personal and ministerial revival, like I had never known before.

Therefore, God, in His faithfulness, at my age of 35, graced me with that kind of unparalleled revival experience. In fact, it was unprecedented, to say the least. Yet that is not all He graciously gave me. In addition to all I have mentioned thus far, God also graced me with the timeless and timely message in this book, as a divine assignment, to preach throughout the United States, Puerto Rico, and Costa Rica, since 2010 until this year.

Now in 2020, in addition to preaching this message, I believe God has added to my assignment, the writing of this book, which will also be translated into Spanish so we can share it in Latin America and beyond. Why? The reason is because God knows how desperately and in dire need is our multiethnic nation for a divine revival now, along with the rest of the multicultural world. In fact, due to this year's unprecedented COVID-19 global pandemic and its detrimental effects on the lives and livelihood of tens of millions of people in our nation and around the world, we cannot afford to have another Great Depression occur resulting in countless of lives and ministers living in grave depression. Additionally, due to the roaring rise of racial tensions in our nation directly related to the recent gross injustices of multiple racial homicides committed by civilians and police officers alike against Black and White Americans, we cannot afford to have a continual increase of this grave depravity. Instead, we must seek God for another Great Awakening that can only come to our nation and beyond through the multicolored Body of Jesus Christ pursuing Him for revival now.

Therefore, in reconnecting to the beginning of this chapter, allow me now to share with you the answer God gave me in 2010 when I asked Him "What is Revival Now?" His complete answer to my question was so extensive that I will need to share it in this chapter and in the next. To begin with, let us consider what God showed me to be the scriptural root of the sacred answer to this timely question. It is registered in Acts 2:1-6, 12-21, and 37-41 which says:

> [1] *When the Day of Pentecost had fully come, they were all with one accord in one place.* [2] *And suddenly there came a sound from heaven, as of a rushing mighty wind, and it filled the whole house where they were sitting.* [3] *Then there appeared to them divided tongues, as of fire, and one sat upon each of them.* [4] *And they were all filled with the Holy Spirit and began to speak with other tongues, as the Spirit gave them utterance.* [5] *And there were dwelling in Jerusalem Jews, devout men, from every nation under heaven.* [6] *And when this sound occurred, the multitude came together, and were confused, because everyone heard them speak in his own language.*
>
> [12] *So they were all amazed and perplexed, saying to one another, "Whatever could this mean?"* [13] *Others mocking said, "They are full of new wine."*
> [14] *But Peter, standing up with the eleven, raised his voice and said to them, "Men of Judea and all who dwell in Jerusalem, let this be known to you, and heed my words.* [15] *For these are not drunk, as you suppose, since it is only the third hour of the day.* [16] *But this is what was spoken by the Prophet Joel:*
> [17] *'And it shall come to pass in the last days, says God, That I will pour out of My Spirit on all flesh; Your sons and your daughters shall prophesy, Your young men shall see visions,*

26

Your old men shall dream dreams.
[18] And on My menservants and on My maidservants
I will pour out My Spirit in those days;
And they shall prophesy.
[19] I will show wonders in heaven above
And signs in the earth beneath:
Blood and fire and vapor of smoke.
[20] The sun shall be turned into darkness,
And the moon into blood,
Before the coming of the great and awesome day of the
LORD.
[21] And it shall come to pass
That whoever calls on the name of the LORD
Shall be saved.'

[37] Now when they heard this, they were cut to the heart, and
said to Peter and the rest of the apostles, "Men and
brethren, what shall we do?"
[38] Then Peter said to them, "Repent, and let every one of
you be baptized in the name of Jesus Christ for the
remission of sins; and you shall receive the gift of the Holy
Spirit. [39] For the promise is to you and to your children, and
to all who are afar off, as many as the Lord our God will
call."
[40] And with many other words he testified and exhorted
them, saying, "Be saved from this perverse generation."
[41] Then those who gladly received his word were baptized;
and that day about three thousand souls were added to
them.

Acts 2:1-6, 12-21, 37-41 NKJV

What a powerful passage of God's word. Can you imagine what it must have been like for the beloved Jewish people who experienced this Jewish festival of Pentecost, which first began at least 1,275 years prior to the time of Acts 2, fifty days after the Israelites were delivered from Egypt on the first Passover? On this particular Pentecost, in the book of Acts, the heavens were opened. God's Holy Spirit was poured out. His beloved Jewish people were filled with His Holy presence, and they were divinely enabled to speak of the wonders of God in fifteen other languages that could be understood by Jews and Gentile converts to Judaism who were visiting Jerusalem from "every nation under heaven." Then, Peter, a disciple of Jesus Christ, who became an apostle for Christ, together with eleven other apostles, stood up to preach God's word for the very first time in his life and ministry. By the time he was done preaching, 3,000 beloved Jews and believing Gentiles turned away from the perversion of their fallen generation and accepted the good news of Jesus Christ, being saved and water baptized. It must have been a glorious experience, and Peter's preaching must have been powerful. In fact, I wholeheartedly believe that what the people experienced in Acts 2 was "revival now," because in essence, "revival now" is what Peter was proclaiming was happening in that place, on that day, with those people of Pentecost.

Allow me to explain. Notice when Peter stood up to preach, he says the following in Acts 2:16:

> *¹⁶ But this is what was spoken by the Prophet Joel:*
>   *Acts 2:16 NKJV*

In this one verse, Peter, in starting to preach his very first message, does not share a funny joke, a world history quote, a personal story, his opinion on a current event, nor anything else like that. Instead, Peter does what he learned, first-hand from our Lord Jesus Christ, during the three years he followed, observed, and listened to Him. What did Peter learn from our Lord? To preach the prophetic word of God and show people how our God is faithful to fulfill His word of prophecy, regardless of how long ago He said He would do something for His people in their future. Just as Jesus Christ focused His life, ministry, and message of God's kingdom, on revealing the fulfillment of the

28

prophecies of the prophets from centuries past, so Peter sought to do the same thing during his first time preaching. Hence, he began preaching by prophetically proclaiming the word of God which revealed God's plan for all mankind to be saved through Jesus Christ. In doing so, he reminded the people in Acts 2 of the biblical prophecy registered in Joel 2:28-32 which says:

> [28] *And it shall come to pass afterward*
> *That I will pour out My Spirit on all flesh;*
> *Your sons and your daughters shall prophesy,*
> *Your old men shall dream dreams,*
> *Your young men shall see visions.*
> [29] *And also on My menservants and on My maidservants*
> *I will pour out My Spirit in those days.*
> [30] *"And I will show wonders in the heavens and in the earth:*
> *Blood and fire and pillars of smoke.*
> [31] *The sun shall be turned into darkness,*
> *And the moon into blood,*
> *Before the coming of the great and awesome day of the*
> *LORD.*
> [32] *And it shall come to pass*
> *That whoever calls on the name of the LORD*
> *Shall be saved.*
> *For in Mount Zion and in Jerusalem there shall be*
> *deliverance,*
> *As the LORD has said,*
> *Among the remnant whom the LORD calls."*
>
> *Joel 2:28-32 NKJV*

Here, Peter, as an apostle, connected his preaching to the prophecy that was given several hundred years prior by the Prophet Joel. Therefore, I believe Peter was proclaiming that the people were experiencing Joel's prophesied future "revival" registered in Joel 2, in Peter's "now" time, revealed in Acts 2. It was "revival now." Why was this happening? The reason is because there comes a time when God's prophetic word must become His apostolic work. In other words, whatever God has foretold about a future time will eventually be fulfilled in a present time. This biblical truth is further emphasized by the Apostle Peter later in the same chapter when he also speaks of David, who was himself a prophet, in addition to being a king, psalmist, and patriarch of Israel.

Correspondingly, Peter reveals to the people that David prophesied hundreds of years before their time of the coming Christ, who would one day in the distant future pour out His Holy Spirit upon His people so they would "now see and hear" what God had promised, according to Acts 2:29-33 which says:

> [29] *Men and brethren, let me speak freely to you of the patriarch David, that he is both dead and buried, and his tomb is with us to this day.* [30] *Therefore, being a prophet, and knowing that God had sworn with an oath to him that of the fruit of his body, according to the flesh, He would raise up the Christ to sit on his throne,* [31] *he, foreseeing this, spoke concerning the resurrection of the Christ, that His soul was not left in Hades, nor did His flesh see corruption.* [32] *This Jesus God has raised up, of which we are all witnesses.* [33] *Therefore being exalted to the right hand of God, and having received from the Father the promise of the Holy Spirit, He poured out this which you now see and hear.*
>
> *Acts 2:29-33 NKJV*

In this passage, the Apostle Peter further reiterates that just as it was with the Prophet Joel, an additional prophecy from the Prophet David, regarding an outpouring of the Holy Spirit resulting in "revival" for God's people, became a reality for the Apostle Peter and the people of God in their "now" time. Therefore, in principle, in order for us to experience a similar and even greater "revival now," we must evolve from the mindset of the Prophet Joel, to the attitude of the Apostle Peter, while maintaining the former as a foundation for our future. While Joel was the prophet who spoke of things to come, Peter became the apostle who saw those things spoken of come to pass. Thus, a prophetic promise must eventually become an apostolic reality.

Why is that? While the prophetic foretells God's word for the future of His people, the apostolic shows God's word fulfilled with miracles, signs, and wonders for His people who behold His presence in their present time. This complementing and culminating distinction can be discovered when we closely observe 2 Peter 1:16-21, Acts 1:21-22, 1 Corinthians 15:3-8, Acts 5:12, and 2 Corinthians 12:12 which say:

> *[16] For we did not follow cunningly devised fables when we made known to you the power and coming of our Lord Jesus Christ, but were eyewitnesses of His majesty. [17] For He received from God the Father honor and glory when such a voice came to Him from the Excellent Glory: "This is My beloved Son, in whom I am well pleased." [18] And we heard this voice which came from heaven when we were with Him on the holy mountain. [19] And so we have the prophetic word confirmed, which you do well to heed as a light that shines in a dark place, until the day dawns and the morning star rises in your hearts; [20] knowing this first, that no prophecy of Scripture is of any private interpretation, [21] for prophecy never came by the will of man, but holy men of God spoke as they were moved by the Holy Spirit.*
>
> *2 Peter 1:16-21 NKJV*

> *[21] Therefore, of these men who have accompanied us all the time that the Lord Jesus went in and out among us,*
> *[22] beginning from the baptism of John to that day when He was taken up from us, one of these must become a witness with us of His resurrection.*
>
> *Acts 1:21-22 NKJV*

31

³ For I delivered to you first of all that which I also received: that Christ died for our sins according to the Scriptures, ⁴ and that He was buried, and that He rose again the third day according to the Scriptures, ⁵ and that He was seen by Cephas, then by the twelve. ⁶ After that He was seen by over five hundred brethren at once, of whom the greater part remain to the present, but some have fallen asleep. ⁷ After that He was seen by James, then by all the apostles. ⁸ Then last of all He was seen by me also, as by one born out of due time.

1 Corinthians 15:3-8 NKJV

¹² And through the hands of the apostles many signs and wonders were done among the people. And they were all with one accord in Solomon's Porch.

Acts 5:12 NKJV

¹² Truly the signs of an apostle were accomplished among you with all perseverance, in signs and wonders and mighty deeds.

2 Corinthians 12:12 NKJV

I repeat, while the prophetic foretells God's word for the future of His people, the apostolic shows God's word fulfilled with miracles, signs, and wonders for His people who behold His presence in their present time. In other words, while the prophetic, so to speak, says in faith, "one of these days, God is going to do…," the apostolic, seeing in faith and beholding in fact, proclaims "this is the day God has done what He said He would do…" Hence, there is a huge complementing, yet distinguishing difference, and I believe God desires for us to see that divine difference become a living reality now in our lives, families, cities, states, nation, and the nations of the world.

32

With that in mind, it is imperative for us to carefully observe the times during which the Prophet Joel and the Apostle Peter ministered in. Doing so will enable us to see what those times can reveal to us. Many biblical scholars believe Joel prophesied in at least 835 B.C., if not further back in time, while all biblical scholars would agree Peter preached in 33 A.D. Therefore, it is believed by many that there was a difference of at least 868 years or more between Joel and Peter, which would be equivalent to almost 9 centuries. Interestingly enough, we should note that in addition to the time difference of approximately 9 centuries between Joel 2 and Acts 2, the disciples and apostles, in Acts 1, were in the upper room for 9 days leading up to the Day of Pentecost. A careful calculation of the amount of days from the Jewish Feasts of Passover to Pentecost, together with an accurate assessment of the days of Jesus' resurrection and ascension, would confirm this. Furthermore, we should note that, according to Acts 2:15, the exact time of day on the Day of Pentecost when the Holy Spirit was poured out upon the believers was 9:00 in the morning.

Now when we combine these numerical observations, we see the common thread of 9's; approximately 9 centuries, 9 days, and 9 in the morning. Was this a mere earthly coincidence or was it a God-incident with a heavenly message? Was this coincidental or providential? I biblically believe it was an intentional God-incident with a providential act of the Divine. Why? In biblical numerology, which is the study of numbers and their significance in the Bible, although the number 9, from an Old Testament Hebrew language perspective, can represent finality, judgement, or completion, 9, from a human and New Testament perspective, can also represent "birthing." This is due to the fact that an expectant woman can safely give birth to a child at 9 months of pregnancy, and that there are 9 fruits of the Holy Spirit which we as Christians are expected to produce, bear or give birth to as a vital sign of our Christian living, according to Galatians 5.

Interestingly enough, the birth of the Church is widely believed by many Biblical scholars to have occurred in Acts 2, which again was approximately 9 centuries from Joel 2, 9 days from the ascension of

Jesus Christ, and occurred at 9 in the morning on the Day of Pentecost. Thus, those three 9's represent a confirmation that what happened on the Day of Pentecost was indeed a birthing of a spoken prophecy that became an apostolic living reality. Therefore, I believe "revival now" is the divine time in which God's prophetic word becomes His Holy Spirit apostolic work, which then births His greater reality for Christ's living church to reach the world it now lives in. In fact, in essence, that is what the Apostle Paul writes about in Romans 8:19-22 which says:

> [19] *For the earnest expectation of the creation eagerly waits for the revealing of the sons of God.* [20] *For the creation was subjected to futility, not willingly, but because of Him who subjected it in hope;* [21] *because the creation itself also will be delivered from the bondage of corruption into the glorious liberty of the children of God.* [22] *For we know that the whole creation groans and labors with birth pangs together until now.*
>
> *Romans 8:19-22 NKJV*

Here we can observe that the Apostle Paul spoke of a time when creation would eagerly expect for God's children to show themselves to this world so humanity would desire to receive what God had already given to His children. Additionally, the climax in this passage is that what God began with His children of past ages would then culminate in the birth pangs of the present age, so a new birth for many more future children of God would happen up until now.

Considering all of this, today, in 2020, almost 20 centuries later after Acts 2, I believe our Lord Jesus Christ has a divine 20/20 vision to see something birthed at an even greater level, dimension, and realm. However, this time, I believe it will not be limited to only happening in one specific city, state, and nation on earth, such as was the case in Acts 2, where it happened in the city of Jerusalem, in the region of Judea, in the nation of Israel. It certainly would be absolutely glorious for it to happen there again.

At the same time, I believe it is God's desire for it to also happen in an unlimited number of cities, states, and nations throughout the world, just so long as there is a people of God in each of those places longing for God to pour out His Holy Spirit upon those places, spaces, and countless of faces. In other words, local revivals must eventually become global revivals. With that in mind, I believe we are on the verge of receiving a global revival now from our Lord Jesus Christ, so the next great awakening can occur. Consequently, it will lead to a greater commitment from the Church to Christ's Great Commission, and the result will be the greatest harvest of souls yet to be seen on earth, before the rapture of the Church and the subsequent Great Tribulation occurs.

How can I be so bold as to believe God for this? The reason, in great part, is because of what God's word collectively says, with regards to this extremely important matter, according to Acts 1:8, Mark 16:15, Matthew 28:18-20, Acts 2:41, Acts 4:4, Acts 17:26-27, Romans 10:8-9, and John 4:35 which say:

[8] But you shall receive power when the Holy Spirit has come upon you; and you shall be witnesses to Me in Jerusalem, and in all Judea and Samaria, and to the end of the earth.

Acts 1:8 NKJV

[15] And He said to them, "Go into all the world and preach the gospel to every creature.

Mark 16:15 NKJV

[18] And Jesus came and spoke to them, saying, "All authority has been given to Me in heaven and on earth. [19] Go therefore and make disciples of all the nations, baptizing them in the name of the Father and of the Son and of the Holy Spirit, [20] teaching them to observe all things that I have commanded you; and lo, I am with you always, even to the end of the age." Amen.

Matthew 28:18-20 NKJV

41 Then those who gladly received his word were baptized; and that day about three thousand souls were added to them.

Acts 2:41 NKJV

4 However, many of those who heard the word believed; and the number of the men came to be about five thousand.

Acts 4:4 NKJV

26 From one man he made all the nations, that they should inhabit the whole earth; and he marked out their appointed times in history and the boundaries of their lands. 27 God did this so that they would seek him and perhaps reach out for him and find him, though he is not far from any one of us.

Acts 17:26-27 NIV

8 But what does it say? "The word is near you, in your mouth and in your heart" (that is, the word of faith which we preach): 9 that if you confess with your mouth the Lord Jesus and believe in your heart that God has raised Him from the dead, you will be saved.

Romans 10:8-9 NKJV

35 Do you not say, 'There are still four months and then comes the harvest'? Behold, I say to you, lift up your eyes and look at the fields, for they are already white for harvest!

John 4:35 NKJV

From these passages of scripture, and the principles they represent in God's kingdom, my faith is stirred to believe God, and our Lord Jesus Christ, for our next great awakening, a greater great commissioning, and the next greatest harvest of souls to be added to Christ's church. Although the nations of the world have been tragically plagued this year with the COVID-19 global pandemic, and although our nation has been tumultuously traumatized by the ever-increasing rise of racial tensions followed by their awful aftermath, I believe our God desires to pour out an awesome global revival pandemic that will cover the earth and reconcile all ethnicities to Him and through Him to one another. In fact, just as Acts 17:26-27 reveals that God has sovereignly set all of humanity in all the nations of the earth for their preappointed times with limited boundaries so the nations would seek and reach out for our Lord Jesus Christ, so I believe now is the time for all the nations of the world to seek for Him, reach out for Him, and find Him, by God's grace and for His glory.

In fact, I wholeheartedly believe that this soon coming outpouring will cover the earth with the knowledge of His glory and the gospel kingdom message of Jesus Christ, according to Habakkuk 2:14 and Matthew 24:14 which say:

> *^{14} For the earth will be filled*
> *With the knowledge of the glory of the LORD,*
> *As the waters cover the sea.*
>
> *Habakkuk 2:14 NKJV*

> *^{14} And this gospel of the kingdom will be preached in all the*
> *world as a witness to all the nations, and then the end will*
> *come.*
>
> *Mathew 24:14 NKJV*

Therefore, global Body of Jesus Christ, it is time for revival now. Multiethnic church of Christ Jesus, can you sense it? Multicolored Christian brothers and sisters, are you ready for it? Multicultural friends in the faith, will you be part of it, or apart from it? I believe you and I will be part of it, and we will receive revival now, so we can release it throughout the world we live in. Yet, for that to happen, I also believe from my personal experience and, more importantly, from the biblical exposition of God's word, that we must acknowledge, understand, and apply to our lives and spheres of influence what God has revealed to me through His word to be the five R's of Revival Now.

1. The REALITY of revival
2. The REMNANT for revival
3. The REVELATION of revival
4. The REASONS for revival
5. The RUDIMENTS of revival

When we acknowledge, understand, and apply these five R's to our lives and spheres of influence, then we will be able to, in addition to ourselves, recruit revivalists and release revival in our nation and beyond. So what do each of these R's mean, and how can we apply them to our lives? I invite and implore you to keep reading this timeless and timely message to find out, and I encourage you to personally pursue our Lord Jesus Christ, more than ever before, as you do. History is in the making for the next great awakening, and its starts with me and you!

CHAPTER 2
IT'S TIME FOR A REALITY CHECK

It's time for a reality check, regarding revival now. In the last chapter, we began answering the question "What is revival now?" In summary, we discovered it is "the divine time in which God's prophetic word becomes His Holy Spirit apostolic work, which then births His greater reality for Christ's living church to reach the world it now lives in." In 2010, this is what God began to show me from Acts 2, as He continued to lead me out of a season of grave depression and into a season of great revival. Yet there was more He had in store to share with me in answer to my question. The additional portion of His answer came to me, through what He showed me to be a much-needed reality check with respect to revival now. Considering the current year and all that has happened and continues to happen around the world and in our nation, due to the COVID-19 global pandemic and the rapidly rising racial tensions across our country, I wholeheartedly believe a reality check about revival is what we need in 2020 and the next decade ahead.

However, what does that actually mean? To begin with, we must clarify what "revival now" is not. Contrary to the negative super-spiritual and impatient connotations the words "revival" and "now" might have for many believers and non-believers alike, such is not the case for the real meaning of "revival now." Therefore, I respectfully submit to you that it is not hype. It is not emotionalism. Neither is it sensationalism. Secondly, we should check what are the real definitions of the words, "revival" and "now." Intriguingly enough, "revival" can have a two-part definition. The first part is "restoration to life" and the second part is "a reawakening of interest in relationship to God." Next, the word "now" also can have a two-part definition. The first part is "the present time or moment" and the second part is "without further delay." To better understand both parts of the two-part definitions for both of these words and how they reveal the second half of the answer to the question at hand, we should take a closer look at both parts of each word and connect them to several passages of God's word. In doing so, we can discover an informed definition that is based on the inspired scriptures of the Bible.

With regards to the word "revival" and its first definition part of "restoration to life," when I initially considered this, the Lord reminded me of what the Apostle Peter wrote in 1 Peter 5:8 which says:

> [8] *Be sober, be vigilant; because your adversary the devil walks about like a roaring lion, seeking whom he may devour.*
>
> *1 Peter 5:8 NKJV*

From this scripture, we can observe the undeniable reality that we need revival, because we do have an adversary, which is Satan, who is like a roaring lion seeking for whom he may devour. This adversary of all humanity seeks to destroy our lives, marriages, families, communities, cities, states, nation, and beyond. In fact, amid the current COVID-19 global pandemic and the present increasing racial unrest in our nation, I believe Satan is doing all he can to utilize this plague and tension among people of all colors to accomplish his diabolic purpose of bringing about destruction to humanity. To that point, the Lord also reminded me of what the Apostle John wrote in John 10:10 which says:

¹⁰ The thief does not come except to steal, and to kill, and to destroy. I have come that they may have life, and that they may have it more abundantly.

John 10:10 NKJV

From this scripture, we should observe and also be thankful for the great news that, although the adversary is like a roaring lion seeking for whom he can devour by stealing, killing, and destroying our lives and much more, Jesus Christ is able to give us life and life more abundantly. Therefore, this in "reality" is "restoration to life." The reason why Christ is able to do this for us is because He is the Lion of the Tribe of Judah, according to Revelation 5:5.

⁵ But one of the elders said to me, "Do not weep. Behold, the Lion of the tribe of Judah, the Root of David, has prevailed to open the scroll and to loose its seven seals."

Revelation 5:5 NKJV

Consequently, it is worth noting that when Jesus Christ restores someone and something, He does not only bring it back to the point at which it once lived before it died. Beyond, and even better than that, He is more than able to take what He restores to an even greater point of living than when it was originally alive, according to Ephesians 3:20 which says:

²⁰ Now to Him who is able to do exceedingly abundantly above all that we ask or think, according to the power that works in us,

Ephesians 3:20 NKJV

Therefore, with all of the attacks of the enemy now taking place against humanity, including God's people, in our nation and throughout the world, I believe it is time for "restoration to life" to occur in our nation and all over the earth. This is a major part of revival. Yet this pertains only to the first part of the definition of "revival."

As I mentioned before, the second part is "a reawakening of interest in relationship to God." When I considered this part, the Lord revealed to me that we need revival, because, unfortunately, the Church of Jesus Christ, generally speaking, has in many ways spiritually fallen asleep and has lost interest in intimately relating to Him. Allow me to explain this with God's word in connection to some post-modern era observations of the Church, especially in the United States. We will start with Revelation 3:1-3 and thereafter move onto Revelation 2:1-5. Consider, first, Revelation 3:1-3 which says:

> *1 "To the angel of the Church in Sardis write:*
> *These are the words of him who holds the seven spirits of*
> *God and the seven stars. I know your deeds; you have a*
> *reputation of being alive, but you are dead. 2 Wake up!*
> *Strengthen what remains and is about to die, for I have*
> *found your deeds unfinished in the sight of my God.*
> *3 Remember, therefore, what you have received and heard;*
> *hold it fast, and repent. But if you do not wake up, I will*
> *come like a thief, and you will not know at what time I will*
> *come to you.*
>
> *Revelation 3:1-3 NIV*

Interestingly enough, according to this passage of scripture, Jesus himself had to address the Church in Sardis to tell them that, although they had a reputation for being alive, they were actually dead, and therefore needed to wake up. In other words, they needed to have a spiritual awakening. Therefore, our post-modern church of today must make sure we do not only have a reputation for being alive, like the Church in Sardis did. Just because we have all sorts of lively and trendy names for our churches, denominations, networks, associations, and so forth, that does not mean we are actually living in the reality and truth of the great names we have. We must truly be alive, by spiritually waking up through a great awakening. Just as Jesus Christ called the Church in Sardis to wake up, I believe He is calling the Church in every nation on earth to wake up and be alive through Him, in Him, and for Him.

Yet that is not all "a reawakening of interest in relationship to God" means, because there is another part to this second part of the definition of revival which has to do with interest in relationship to God. Before I address this, let us consider Revelation 2:1-5 which says:

> [1] *"To the angel of the Church of Ephesus write,*
> *'These things says He who holds the seven stars in His right*
> *hand, who walks in the midst of the seven golden*
> *lampstands:* [2] *"I know your works, your labor, your*
> *patience, and that you cannot bear those who are evil. And*
> *you have tested those who say they are apostles and are not,*
> *and have found them liars;* [3] *and you have persevered and*
> *have patience, and have labored for My name's sake and*
> *have not become weary.* [4] *Nevertheless I have this against*
> *you, that you have left your first love.* [5] *Remember therefore*
> *from where you have fallen; repent and do the first works,*
> *or else I will come to you quickly and remove your*
> *lampstand from its place—unless you repent."*
>
> Revelation 2:1-5 NKJV

Intriguingly enough, according to this passage of scripture, Jesus Christ himself has to address the Church in Ephesus to let them know, although they had a lot of good works or religious practices, they had actually abandoned the most important thing, which was their first love towards Him. In other words, just because the Church in Ephesus had good religion, it did not mean it had a great relationship. Unfortunately, I believe the same can be said of the Church in our nation and around the world during our post-modern era. Therefore, we should ask, what is the difference, or distinction, between a good religion and a great relationship?

Let us consider both words of "religion" and "relationship." The word "religion" is comprised of the two parts of "re" and "ligion." These parts of this word implies "the act of repeating laws" in an attempt to obtain a right standing with God, specifically Jesus Christ, in this case. However, the word "relationship" is comprised of the two parts of "re" and "lationship." which is quite different. These two parts imply "the affectionate repetition of a heartbeat" in an attraction of being obsessed with Jesus Christ and desiring to become one with Him. We can know this because the "lation" portion of this word derives from the Latin and Spanish word of "latir" which literally means "heartbeat." Additionally, the suffix of this word, "ship," implies a degree of great size, like a ship that is much larger than a boat or even a yacht. Therefore, while religion can be a good thing in terms of the Church repeatedly observing the laws in God's word in hopes of us being right before Jesus Christ, a relationship carries the far greater reality of having a heart that beats repeatedly in love for Jesus Christ, as a result of us being totally obsessed with Him and desiring to be one with Him. This reminds me of my initial and ongoing personal experiences with Mildred, which helps me understand the difference between religion and relationship.

When I first saw Mildred, in the Summer of 1993, in Rochester, NY, at a youth and young adult gathering at the home of our dear friends Abdy and Omayra Sellas, something happened to my heart rate. Once I noticed Mildred, my heart began to accelerate because I was attracted to her. Then, soon thereafter, when we officially met at a youth and young adult worship service and eventually began to date each other, every time I saw her, my heart would beat faster. Moreover, when I asked her to marry me about two years later, my heart would beat even faster. Finally, when about one year later, on our wedding day of Saturday, March 16, 1996, we said "I do" to each other, my heart beat faster than it had ever beaten before in my life. Why? I had a relationship, not a religion, with Mildred. Correspondingly, I believe there is a parallel application in this analogy for the Church of Jesus Christ and the Christ of the Church. It applies to both the Church in Ephesus during its time and also to the worldwide church in our post-modern times.

Today's church has to be extremely careful that we do not only have good works or godly religious practices. We must also make sure that even greater than our good works and godly religion is our divine spiritual relationship with Jesus Christ. In order for this to happen, we must return to our first love with Him, just as He told the Church of Ephesus they needed to do so. In fact, I believe today's post-modern church needs to not only return to our first love with Christ. In addition, we must increase even more in love with Him. This is of utmost importance for the Church, because when Jesus Christ returns for His church, He will return for more than just a church body, fellowship, network, association, denomination, and so forth. In fact, Christ will return for the Body of Christ which, biblically speaking, has been betrothed to Him as His bride who will celebrate the wedding supper of the Lamb with Him, according to Revelation 19:6-9 and Revelation 22:17 which say:

> *6 Then I heard what sounded like a great multitude, like the roar of rushing waters and like loud peals of thunder, shouting:*
> *"Hallelujah!*
> *   For our Lord God Almighty reigns.*
> *7 Let us rejoice and be glad*
> *   and give him glory!*
> *For the wedding of the Lamb has come,*
> *   and his bride has made herself ready.*
> *8 Fine linen, bright and clean,*
> *   was given her to wear."*
> *(Fine linen stands for the righteous acts of God's holy people.)*
> *9 Then the angel said to me, "Write this: Blessed are those who are invited to the wedding supper of the Lamb!" And he added, "These are the true words of God."*
> *   Revelation 19:6-9 NIV*

¹⁷ And the Spirit and the bride say, "Come!" And let him who hears say, "Come!" And let him who thirsts come. Whoever desires, let him take the water of life freely.

Revelation 22:17 NKJV

In addition to these scriptures, the profound revelation that the Church is indeed the bride of Jesus Christ is previously revealed in the Bible in additional scriptural passages such as John 3:27-30 and Ephesians 5:30-32 which say:

²⁷ John answered and said, "A man can receive nothing unless it has been given to him from heaven. ²⁸ You yourselves bear me witness, that I said, 'I am not the Christ,' but, 'I have been sent before Him.' ²⁹ He who has the bride is the bridegroom; but the friend of the bridegroom, who stands and hears him, rejoices greatly because of the bridegroom's voice. Therefore this joy of mine is fulfilled. ³⁰ He must increase, but I must decrease.

John 3:27-30 NKJV

³⁰ For we are members of His body, of His flesh and of His bones. ³¹ "For this reason a man shall leave his father and mother and be joined to his wife, and the two shall become one flesh." ³² This is a great mystery, but I speak concerning Christ and the Church.

Ephesians 5:30-32 NKJV

In these scriptures, we can see that the Apostles John and Paul refer to the Church or body of believers as a bride who belongs to the bridegroom, who is Jesus Christ. In fact, I believe we are headed for a great bridal revival that will result in a great dance of romance between Christ, the Bridegroom, and the Church as the bride of Christ. Therefore, I believe it is Christ's desire to release a romantic revival on His beloved church. Evidence of this prophetic Messianic marriage is also revealed and registered in Song of Solomon 8:1-7, in which the Shulamite woman, who prophetically represents the bride of Christ, says the following to King Solomon, who prophetically represents Jesus Christ, the Bridegroom:

¹ Oh, that you were like my brother,
Who nursed at my mother's breasts!
If I should find you outside,
I would kiss you;
I would not be despised.
² I would lead you and bring you
Into the house of my mother,
She who used to instruct me.
I would cause you to drink of spiced wine,
Of the juice of my pomegranate.
³ His left hand is under my head,
And his right hand embraces me.
⁴ I charge you, O daughters of Jerusalem,
Do not stir up nor awaken love
Until it pleases.
⁵ Who is this coming up from the wilderness,
Leaning upon her beloved?
I awakened you under the apple tree.
There your mother brought you forth;
There she who bore you brought you forth.
⁶ Set me as a seal upon your heart,
As a seal upon your arm;
For love is as strong as death,
Jealousy as cruel as the grave;
Its flames are flames of fire,
A most vehement flame.
⁷ Many waters cannot quench love,
Nor can the floods drown it.
If a man would give for love

All the wealth of his house,
It would be utterly despised.

Song of Solomon 8:1-7 NKJV

This prophetic messianic marriage and romantic revival sentiment is the climax of what is registered and revealed throughout the majority of Song of Solomon in the following scriptural citations, 2:1-17; 3:1-11; 4:1-16; 5:1-16; 7:1-13. Why is this? I believe the reason is because Jesus Christ desires for His church to be divinely stirred and spiritually awakened to a more intimate relationship with Him. In fact, when we consider that in the last chapter of this book, we discovered revival has to do with the concept of birthing, it is worth mentioning that, in order for there to be a birthing, there must first be a conception, and a conception cannot occur without intimacy.

Correspondingly, Christ, the Bridegroom, is calling the Church, His bride, to return to its first love for him, more than ever before. Needless to say, it is high time for the Church to be stirred up in love. In fact, as the Church, we must be awakened, quickened, and revived in love, but not with just any kind of love. Specifically speaking, it must be the kind of first love that continues to grow increasingly stronger as the time of our messianic marriage with Jesus Christ draws closer and closer.

Therefore, the Church must have a reawakening of interest in relationship to God, namely Jesus Christ. Now is not the time for the Church to be asleep, while the Bridegroom prepares to return for His bride, as noted in the parable of the ten virgins in Matthew 25:1-13 which says:

> [1] *At that time the kingdom of heaven will be like ten virgins who took their lamps and went out to meet the bridegroom.* [2] *Five of them were foolish and five were wise.* [3] *The foolish ones took their lamps but did not take any oil with them.* [4] *The wise ones, however, took oil in jars along with their lamps.* [5] *The bridegroom was a long time in coming, and they all became drowsy and fell asleep.*

6 "At midnight the cry rang out: 'Here's the bridegroom! Come out to meet him!'

7 "Then all the virgins woke up and trimmed their lamps.

8 The foolish ones said to the wise, 'Give us some of your oil; our lamps are going out.'

9 "'No,' they replied, 'there may not be enough for both us and you. Instead, go to those who sell oil and buy some for yourselves.'

10 "But while they were on their way to buy the oil, the bridegroom arrived. The virgins who were ready went in with him to the wedding banquet. And the door was shut.

11 "Later the others also came. 'Lord, Lord,' they said, 'open the door for us!'

12 "But he replied, 'Truly I tell you, I don't know you.'

13 "Therefore keep watch, because you do not know the day or the hour."

Matthew 25:1-13 NIV

Consequently, we, as Christ's bride, must be reawakened in interest in relationship to Christ, who is our Beloved Bridegroom. He is coming soon and we must get ready now for His eminent return.

Speaking of getting ready now, since we have discovered the reality of what the word "revival" means in its two-part form, we must move onto checking what the definition is for the word "now." This will help us greatly in our quest to fully define "revival now" and experience a reality check. As you might recall, from earlier in this chapter, the word "now" has two parts to its definition. The first part means "the present time or moment." Back in 2010, when I first considered that portion, the Lord reminded me of Acts 2:1-2 and thereafter drew my attention to Acts 2:32-33. Consider what they reveal to us about the word "now" which on one hand means "the present time or moment."

1 When the Day of Pentecost had fully come, they were all with one accord in one place. 2 And suddenly there came a

49

sound from heaven, as of a rushing mighty wind, and it
filled the whole house where they were sitting.

Acts 2:1-2 NKJV

[32] *This Jesus God has raised up, of which we are all*
witnesses. [33] *Therefore being exalted to the right hand of*
God, and having received from the Father the promise of
the Holy Spirit, He poured out this which you now see and
hear.

Acts 2:32-33 NKJV

Interestingly enough, when the Day of Pentecost had arrived, the Apostle Peter and the 120 disciples who were with him arrived to a "present time or moment" set by God, which was 9 in the morning. Peter refers to that hour as a "now" time based on the prophecy of David, the patriarch. That particular "present time or moment" was of utmost importance. I believe this to be the case, because their moment with God resulted in a momentum from God, which led to a movement of God, bringing about an impact from God and climaxing into a world-change for God's glory. Likewise, I believe such can be the case for us today in our present time or moment. Allow me to further explain why I believe this. I have learned from my personal revival experience, in addition to my biblical exegetical study, that a moment with God can produce a divine momentum, movement, impact, and world change from God.

How so, you might ask? Consider that the word "moment" is the root word of "momentum." This observation reveals we must first have a moment with God, before we can receive momentum from God. Otherwise, without a moment with God, all we would have is an "...um" without God. That would be the polar opposite of a "momentum" from God. Additionally, as it pertains to receiving a "movement from God," there must first be a person or a group of people who will cry out "move me, God." Otherwise, the word "movement" without its two-word prefix of "move-me" would only be an "nt", which makes no vernacular sense at all. If anything, the only thing an "nt" might imply in the English language is the suffix "n't", which is placed on the back end of words such as "haven't" which would mean "have not." This reveals that if you and I do not cry out to God to "move me," then we will "not" have a "move-me-nt" from God. Therefore we must experience a personal moment with God to receive momentum from God. Additionally, we must each ask Him to "move me" in order to receive His movement for each of us. When we do so, then we will also experience His impact in our lives that will result in a world-change for our lives and the lives of those around us.

Furthermore, as it pertains to defining the word "now" and considering the second part of this word, we should consider the meaning of "without further delay." When the Day of Pentecost had arrived, the 120 disciples could not afford to wait any longer for, nor further delay, Christ's promised Holy Spirit. I believe the reason for this was because what they received from the Lord in their moment with Him on the Day of Pentecost would, soon thereafter, exponentially impact their present time and future seasons. In other words, God had a set time for the 120 disciples in the upper room that directly influenced His set time for the 3,000 new believers on the Temple Mount, which eventually impacted the 5,000 men that were added to the Church in Acts 4:4, due to God's sequentially set time for them all. Therefore, I believe that such is the case for us today. We cannot afford to put off any further, nor further delay, God's move in our lives that will impact us and those around us in our present time and seasons ahead. In fact, I wholeheartedly believe what God will do to us and through us in 2020 will greatly impact our nation and our world not only for the rest of this year, but also for the next 10 years. This is what God revealed to me in 2008 to be "accelerated timing for an exponential impact," which I wrote about in my first book, "Now is the Time."

Consequently, in conclusion and in consideration of all we have covered in this chapter, when I reflect on the two-part definitions of the two words of "revival" and "now," I believe the following additional definition for "revival now" is evident. "Revival Now" is the divine restoration to life that can only result from a reawakening of interest in relationship to Jesus Christ, which is needed at the present time and moment without any further delay. Now with that in mind, let us believe God for revival now and discover in the next chapter how we can become a real remnant of revival that He desires to revive and revive others through. History is in the making for the next great awakening, and the reality check of revival must be realized by me and you!

CHAPTER 3
THERE IS A REAL REMNANT

Every revival requires a real remnant of revivalists. This is one of the key things I have learned about revival from my personal experience and biblical exegetical study on the matter. In fact, Mildred and I experienced this first-hand in San Antonio, in 2010, with our dear friends, Eileen Vincent and Natalie Hardy of City Reachers, and with our dear friends, Pastor Nino Gonzalez and Worship Leader Bryan Apodaca of Cornerstone Church's High School Youth Ministry, during that time. Between the core groups of multiethnic believers who attended the weekly Friday Night City Reachers Prayer Meetings, and the multicolored volunteer leaders of the Cornerstone High School Youth Ministry we led in that season of ministry, these two groups of people became a real remnant of revivalists who dared to believe God for "revival now" and who had accepted the corresponding reality check spoken of in the previous chapter.

Together, we expected for revival to be poured out upon us and all those around us during that particular season of great awakening. Just imagine what will happen in the latter part of this 2020 year and throughout the next decade, as the multiethnic, multicolored, and multicultural Body of Jesus Christ begins to do the same in our nation and around the world. Regardless of the continued effects of the COVID-19 global pandemic and the rising racial tensions in our nation, indeed, history will continue to be in the making for the next great awakening. I believe this to be true, not only because of what we personally experienced in 2010, but more importantly because of what the Bible shows the 120 disciples, in Acts 2, supernaturally experienced approximately 2,000 years ago on the Day of Pentecost. Consider verses 12-21 which say:

> [12] *So they were all amazed and perplexed, saying to one another, "Whatever could this mean?"* [13] *Others mocking said, "They are full of new wine."*
> [14] *But Peter, standing up with the eleven, raised his voice and said to them, "Men of Judea and all who dwell in Jerusalem, let this be known to you, and heed my words.*
> [15] *For these are not drunk, as you suppose, since it is only the third hour of the day.* [16] *But this is what was spoken by the Prophet Joel:*
> [17] *'And it shall come to pass in the last days, says God, That I will pour out of My Spirit on all flesh; Your sons and your daughters shall prophesy, Your young men shall see visions, Your old men shall dream dreams.*
> [18] *And on My menservants and on My maidservants I will pour out My Spirit in those days; And they shall prophesy.*
> [19] *I will show wonders in heaven above And signs in the earth beneath: Blood and fire and vapor of smoke.*
> [20] *The sun shall be turned into darkness, And the moon into blood, Before the coming of the great and awesome day of the* LORD.

²¹ And it shall come to pass
That whoever calls on the name of the LORD
Shall be saved.'

Acts 2:12-21 NKJV

In this passage of scripture, the Apostle Peter is not preaching alone. Rather, he stands up with eleven other apostles who are part of a group of 120 disciples who are being questioned about the outpouring of the Holy Spirit they had just received. This group of 120 disciples was significant for many reasons, including one reason which reveals that they were a remnant of believers as prophesied about in Joel 2:28-32. For the sake of brevity, let us only consider verse 32 which says:

³² And it shall come to pass
That whoever calls on the name of the LORD
Shall be saved.
For in Mount Zion and in Jerusalem there shall be
deliverance,
As the LORD has said,
Among the remnant whom the LORD calls.

Joel 2:32 NKJV

In this passage of scripture, we see that Joel specifically prophesied about a remnant. Therefore, since Peter proclaimed the outpouring of the Holy Spirit was an apostolic fulfillment of Joel's prophecy, we can understand that the group of 120 disciples was indeed a remnant. In fact, I believe they were a real remnant of revivalists who serve as an example for other believers to follow during our post-modern times. Just as Acts 2 and Joel 2 jointly reveal that God revived a remnant of believers in order to revive others through their lives, I believe God is now seeking for a remnant which represents the rest of the Body of Jesus Christ and those believers who will be added to Christ's church through their Christian testimony and witness of Jesus Christ. I say this because by definition a remnant is a small piece or portion of a material or a group of people which represents the rest of the material or group which is being considered, such as in the case of fabric or carpet. In other words, a fabric or carpet remnant can be a square-inch sample that reflects what the rest of the square-feet of the fabric or carpet looks and actually is like. Correspondingly, in terms of a revival remnant of people, it is a small portion of a larger group of people that needs revival which includes our families, communities, cities, states, nation, and beyond.

Therefore, I believe God is searching for a revival remnant of modern-day Peter's and disciples, like the 120 disciples who went to the upper room before they impacted 3,000 people on the Day of Pentecost and thereafter impacted many more thousands of people. This revival remnant is like the 120 of the 500 believers who Jesus Christ appeared to after His resurrection. These 120 are the ones who obeyed Christ's instruction for them to go to the upper room, instead of the 380 that possibly received the same invitation from Christ, but perhaps chose to stay at home in their own rooms instead for whatever reasons. I believe this to be the case based on 1 Corinthians 15:3-6 and Acts 1:4, 12-15 which say:

> *3 For I delivered to you first of all that which I also received: that Christ died for our sins according to the Scriptures, 4 and that He was buried, and that He rose again the third day according to the Scriptures, 5 and that He was seen by Cephas, then by the twelve. 6 After that He was seen by over five hundred brethren at once, of whom the greater part remain to the present, but some have fallen asleep.*
>
> *1 Corinthians 15:3-6 NKJV*

> *4 And being assembled together with them, He commanded them not to depart from Jerusalem, but to wait for the Promise of the Father, "which," He said, "you have heard from Me;*

*¹² Then they returned to Jerusalem from the mount called
Olivet, which is near Jerusalem, a Sabbath day's journey.
¹³ And when they had entered, they went up into the upper
room where they were staying: Peter, James, John, and
Andrew; Philip and Thomas; Bartholomew and Matthew;
James the son of Alphaeus and Simon the Zealot; and Judas
the son of James. ¹⁴ These all continued with one accord in
prayer and supplication, with the women and Mary the
mother of Jesus, and with His brothers.
¹⁵ And in those days Peter stood up in the midst of the
disciples (altogether the number of names was about a
hundred and twenty), and said,*

Acts 1:4, 12-15 NKJV

These passages of scripture collectively reveal to us there was
indeed a real remnant of revivalists. In fact, they were real in more ways
than one. On one hand, they really did exist, and on the other hand, they
were real people, with imperfections and all, just like Peter the preacher
of Pentecost. I say this because when we consider the life of Peter, we
can understand that modern-day Peter's are real people who are not
humanly perfect, but are in hot pursuit of God's perfecting presence. This
can be observed in the life of Peter as expressed in Matthew 14:25-31,
Matthew 16:13-23 and Luke 22:29-34, 59-62 which say:

*²⁵ Now in the fourth watch of the night Jesus went to them,
walking on the sea. ²⁶ And when the disciples saw Him
walking on the sea, they were troubled, saying, "It is a
ghost!" And they cried out for fear.
²⁷ But immediately Jesus spoke to them, saying, "Be of good
cheer! It is I; do not be afraid."
²⁸ And Peter answered Him and said, "Lord, if it is You,
command me to come to You on the water."
²⁹ So He said, "Come." And when Peter had come down out
of the boat, he walked on the water to go to Jesus. ³⁰ But*

*when he saw that the wind was boisterous, he was afraid;
and beginning to sink he cried out, saying, "Lord, save
me!"*

*[31] And immediately Jesus stretched out His hand and caught
him, and said to him, "O you of little faith, why did you
doubt?"*

Matthew 14:25-31 NKJV

*[13] When Jesus came to the region of Caesarea Philippi, he
asked his disciples, "Who do people say the Son of Man
is?"*

*[14] They replied, "Some say John the Baptist; others say
Elijah; and still others, Jeremiah or one of the prophets."*

*[15] "But what about you?" he asked. "Who do you say I
am?"*

*[16] Simon Peter answered, "You are the Messiah, the Son of
the living God."*

*[17] Jesus replied, "Blessed are you, Simon son of Jonah, for
this was not revealed to you by flesh and blood, but by my
Father in heaven. [18] And I tell you that you are Peter, and
on this rock I will build my church, and the gates of Hades
will not overcome it. [19] I will give you the keys of the
kingdom of heaven; whatever you bind on earth will be
bound in heaven, and whatever you loose on earth will be
loosed in heaven." [20] Then he ordered his disciples not to
tell anyone that he was the Messiah.*

*[21] From that time on Jesus began to explain to his disciples
that he must go to Jerusalem and suffer many things at the
hands of the elders, the chief priests and the teachers of the
law, and that he must be killed and on the third day be
raised to life.*

*[22] Peter took him aside and began to rebuke him. "Never,
Lord!" he said. "This shall never happen to you!"*

23 Jesus turned and said to Peter, "Get behind me, Satan! You are a stumbling block to me; you do not have in mind the concerns of God, but merely human concerns."

Matthew 16:13-23 NIV

29 And I confer on you a kingdom, just as my Father conferred one on me, 30 so that you may eat and drink at my table in my kingdom and sit on thrones, judging the twelve tribes of Israel.
31 "Simon, Simon, Satan has asked to sift all of you as wheat. 32 But I have prayed for you, Simon, that your faith may not fail. And when you have turned back, strengthen your brothers."
33 But he replied, "Lord, I am ready to go with you to prison and to death."
34 Jesus answered, "I tell you, Peter, before the rooster crows today, you will deny three times that you know me."

59 About an hour later another asserted, "Certainly this fellow was with him, for he is a Galilean."
60 Peter replied, "Man, I don't know what you're talking about!" Just as he was speaking, the rooster crowed. 61 The Lord turned and looked straight at Peter. Then Peter remembered the word the Lord had spoken to him: "Before the rooster crows today, you will disown me three times."
62 And he went outside and wept bitterly.

Luke 22:29-34, 59-62 NIV

These three passages of scripture jointly reveal just how real Peter was, as a human being who was having supernatural experiences with Jesus Christ. During one moment, he was walking on water while having his focus on Jesus, but in the next moment he was sinking in the same water because he had taken his focus off of Jesus. On another occasion, Peter was receiving revelation from our Heavenly Father regarding Jesus being the Christ, but in the next moment he was being influenced by Satan against Jesus Christ. Additionally, on yet another occasion, Peter was being divinely promoted by Christ Jesus together with the other apostles, but soon thereafter, he was denying Christ while being distant from the other apostles.

In other words, Peter was not perfect by any stretch of the imagination, and he struggled with his humanity just like real people do, including me and you. I share this, not to be judgmental towards Peter, nor to discourage modern-day Peter's from becoming a real remnant of revivalists, but rather to be compassionate and encouraging towards them so they can come into being a remnant of revivalists who are for real. In fact, this modern-day Peter-like revival remnant is one that desires to be real with God and experience the realness of God. So much so that it does not matter how imperfect modern-day revivalists like Peter are, because God is able to gracefully revive them and revive others through them. In fact, I believe God is presently searching for a real remnant of modern-day revivalists, like Peter, who will be revived by Him, so God can then revive others through them, as noted in John 21:15-17 and Acts 2:40-41 which say:

> [15] So when they had eaten breakfast, Jesus said to Simon Peter, "Simon, son of Jonah, do you love Me more than these?"
> He said to Him, "Yes, Lord; You know that I love You."
> He said to him, "Feed My lambs."
> [16] He said to him again a second time, "Simon, son of Jonah, do you love Me?"
> He said to Him, "Yes, Lord; You know that I love You."
> He said to him, "Tend My sheep."
> [17] He said to him the third time, "Simon, son of Jonah, do you love Me?" Peter was grieved because He said to him the third time, "Do you love Me?"
> And he said to Him, "Lord, You know all things; You know that I love You."

John 21:15-17 NKJV

[40] And with many other words he testified and exhorted them, saying, "Be saved from this perverse generation." [41] Then those who gladly received his word were baptized; and that day about three thousand souls were added to them.

Acts 2:40-41 NKJV

In these passages of scripture we see that when Peter was revived by Jesus Christ in John 21, although the revival started with him, it did not stop with him. Instead, the revival came to Peter so that it could flow through Peter into the lives of many others who were just like him, including the other eleven apostles, the rest of the 120 disciples, and the 3,000 converts mentioned in Acts 1 and 2. Today, the great news is that every believer has the potential to become a modern-day real revivalist like Peter. In fact, this is scripturally substantiated when we consider God's word in 1 Peter 2:1-10 which says:

[1] Therefore, rid yourselves of all malice and all deceit, hypocrisy, envy, and slander of every kind. [2] Like newborn babies, crave pure spiritual milk, so that by it you may grow up in your salvation, [3] now that you have tasted that the Lord is good.
[4] As you come to him, the living Stone—rejected by humans but chosen by God and precious to him— [5] you also, like living stones, are being built into a spiritual house to be a holy priesthood, offering spiritual sacrifices acceptable to God through Jesus Christ. [6] For in Scripture it says:
"See, I lay a stone in Zion,
   a chosen and precious cornerstone,
and the one who trusts in him
   will never be put to shame."

⁷ Now to you who believe, this stone is precious. But to those who do not believe,
"The stone the builders rejected
has become the cornerstone,"
⁸ and,
"A stone that causes people to stumble
and a rock that makes them fall."
They stumble because they disobey the message—which is also what they were destined for.
⁹ But you are a chosen people, a royal priesthood, a holy nation, God's special possession, that you may declare the praises of him who called you out of darkness into his wonderful light. ¹⁰ Once you were not a people, but now you are the people of God; once you had not received mercy, but now you have received mercy.

I Peter 2:1-10 NIV

In this passage of scripture, Peter himself biblically reveals that even new born believers, who at one time had not been God's people, can now become God's people through His great mercy which can make them to become living stones connected to the Living and Chief Cornerstone, which is Christ Himself. In other words, there is hope for all of God's people to become His real remnant of revivalists. Subsequently, I wholeheartedly believe we can all be the modern-day Peter-like real revivalists God is presently searching to revive and bring revival through to many others.

Moreover, when I biblically consider the revival remnant Peter represents, I also believe it is very important we remember it was primarily a generation within a specific age-range. What am I referring to, and what was the predominant age group of Peter and the other apostles who led the 120 into the upper room? Contrary to popular belief, it is a generation that is much younger than many people think. To help us understand this, we should consider Matthew 17:24-27 which says:

^{24} When they had come to Capernaum, those who received the temple tax came to Peter and said, "Does your Teacher not pay the temple tax?"
^{25} He said, "Yes."
And when he had come into the house, Jesus anticipated him, saying, "What do you think, Simon? From whom do the kings of the earth take customs or taxes, from their sons or from strangers?"
^{26} Peter said to Him, "From strangers."
Jesus said to him, "Then the sons are free. ^{27} Nevertheless, lest we offend them, go to the sea, cast in a hook, and take the fish that comes up first. And when you have opened its mouth, you will find a piece of money; take that and give it to them for Me and you."

Matthew 17:24-27 NKJV

Now what does this passage have anything to do with revealing the specific age-range of a generation of revivalists? Let us consider this passage. Peter was asked by Jesus about whether or not Jesus, Peter, and the other disciples were supposed to pay temple taxes. Jesus' response was "no," due to them being sons of the King, who in this case would have been their Heavenly Father. However, Jesus decided to pay temple taxes, regardless, so as to not go against their taxation system. He tells Peter to go cast his fishing line, catch the first fish, and take out of its mouth a Greek four-drachmas coin, which was equal to one Jewish shekel. This miracle was done so Peter could pay taxes for Jesus and himself, since each Jewish person had to pay a half-shekel for the temple taxes. Why was this the case and where did this originate from? The answers to those questions are found in the Old Testament, which teaches that the temple taxes were only paid by those who were age twenty and older. This can be observed in Exodus 30:13-14 which says:

^{13} This is what everyone among those who are numbered shall give: half a shekel according to the shekel of the

sanctuary (a shekel is twenty gerahs). The half-shekel shall
be an offering to the LORD. [14] Everyone included among
those who are numbered, from twenty years old and above,
shall give an offering to the LORD.

Exodus 30:13-14 NKJV

Yet you might wonder, what does this reveal about the age-range of the revival remnant generation of Peter's day? We know according to Luke 3:23, Jesus started his ministry at about age 30.

[23] Now Jesus Himself began His ministry at about thirty
years of age, being (as was supposed) the son of Joseph, the
son of Heli,

Luke 3:23 NKJV

Yet, we do not know exactly how old Peter and the other disciples were at the time of the gospels and the beginning of the book of Acts. However, we do understand this passage reveals that Peter had to have been at least 20 years of age, since he had to pay temple taxes along with Jesus. Therefore, Peter was a young adult. What this passage also indirectly reveals is the age-range of the other disciples who were in Matthew 17, but were not included in the miracle Jesus did in order to pay temple taxes for those who needed to pay them according to the Jewish law. Hence, what were the ages of the other disciples, besides Peter? Their ages had to have been below 20 years of age. Additionally, Jewish rabbinical tradition reveals Rabbi's would wait until young men turned 13 years of age, before recruiting them to become their disciples or students. One reason for this was because by that time the young boys would have memorized the Torah or Pentateuch, which are the first five books of the Bible. The other reason is because after age 13, young men would then have begun to enter into their future trade or profession.

Now with this in mind, what does this reveal to us? This reveals that, in Matthew 17, Peter was in his twenties and the rest of the disciples, who were mentioned earlier in the same chapter were between the ages of 13 and 19. Therefore, I believe the Bible reveals that the age-range of Christ's disciples who were the leaders of the revival remnant generation of Peter's day were primarily youth and young adults. It was this young generation that God revived in order to bring revival to the lives of many others. Correspondingly, I wholeheartedly believe God now seeks to do the same thing again in our day with a young generation of modern-day Peter's who are a real remnant of revival.

In fact, this reminds me of how God did this very thing with a young generation 116 years ago, during the 1904-05 Welsh Revival, through the life of a 26-year old revivalist named Evan Roberts. He was a coal miner who had a late start in going to Bible college. Leading up to and during his first semester of his first year of Bible school, he experienced a personal revival that flowed through his life into the lives of seventeen other youth and young adults in his local church in Loughor, Wales. Eventually, what began as a youth and young adult revival became a country wide revival that impacted the world, and what continued as a local great awakening for young adults culminated in a global great awakening for adults of all ages. In fact, it is believed by credible historians of revival history that the 1904-05 Welsh Revival and the prayers of Evan Roberts contributed greatly to the 1906 Azusa Street Revival in Los Angeles, California.

How so, you might ask? Revival history reveals that a Pastor by the name of Joseph Smale of First Baptist Church, in Los Angeles, went to Wales in 1905 to personally experience the Welsh Revival and then returned to Los Angeles with a desire to experience revival in his own city. Consequently a periodic visitor to his church services, by the name of Frank Bartleman, would periodically write letters to Evan Roberts requesting prayer for the revival in Wales to come to Los Angeles, California and beyond. This is especially noteworthy because Frank Bartleman, who was an Anglo American, became the journalists of, and one of the key contributors to, the 1906 Azusa Street Revival led by William Seymour, who was an African American. On an extremely important side note amid the current rising racial tensions in our nation, I love the fact that God sovereignly utilized two Christian black and white men to work together in what became a multiethnic revival for the city of Los Angeles, the state of California, and the nation of the United States of America. Now with regards to Bartleman's letters to Roberts, Roberts replied with at least three letters expressing his commitment to join Bartleman in praying for revival, and the rest is history – revival history that is.

With that said, I believe Evan Roberts was a modern-day Peter of his time. He was a young adult who was far from perfect, but was nevertheless constantly drawing nearer to the heart of God, to the mind of Christ, and to the presence of the Holy Spirit. Robert's personal revival, as a young adult, resulted in a small corporate youth and young adult remnant of revivalists who God revived countless of others through in their country and beyond. Their young adult local revival eventually climaxed into a global revival for adults of all ages.

Now what does that have to do with the youth and young adults of our modern time? Perhaps everything and much more than we think. I say this because I wholeheartedly believe the young people of today are the modern-day Peter's of the real revival remnant in our time who God desires to bring revival to and through for their generation and beyond. Consequently, just as Roberts was noted for praying the simple, yet profound prayer of "Lord, bend me"[1] in 1904, now in 2020 and onward, I believe this new generation will pray another simple, yet profound prayer of "Lord, shake me 'till you wake me." This prayer is based on Hebrews 12:25-29 and Haggai 2:6-9 which say:

> [25] *See that you do not refuse Him who speaks. For if they did not escape who refused Him who spoke on earth, much more shall we not escape if we turn away from Him who speaks from heaven,* [26] *whose voice then shook the earth; but now He has promised, saying, "Yet once more I shake not only the earth, but also heaven." [27] Now this, "Yet once more," indicates the removal of those things that are being shaken, as of things that are made, that the things which cannot be shaken may remain.*

²⁸ Therefore, since we are receiving a kingdom which cannot be shaken, let us have grace, by which we may serve God acceptably with reverence and godly fear. ²⁹ For our God is a consuming fire.

Hebrews 12:25-29 NKJV

⁶ For thus says the LORD of hosts: "Once more (it is a little while) I will shake heaven and earth, the sea and dry land; ⁷ and I will shake all nations, and they shall come to the Desire of All Nations, and I will fill this temple with glory," says the LORD of hosts. ⁸ "The silver is Mine, and the gold is Mine," says the LORD of hosts. ⁹ "The glory of this latter temple shall be greater than the former," says the LORD of hosts. "And in this place I will give peace," says the LORD of hosts.

Haggai 2:6-9 NKJV

Yes, now more than ever before, we need a real remnant of revival that will cry out to God in prayer "Lord, shake me 'till you wake me!" Subsequently, I believe the revival that God will respond with, which is also known as a Great Awakening, will be greater than those of the past, and His glory and peace will cover the earth like never before. In fact, in faith believing all of God's word that has been shared in this book until now, I dare to declare that this revival will be all about the fullness of God's glorious kingdom brought forth from Heaven to Earth. I also believe it will not be limited to a specific expression of revival noted mainly for salvations or healings or deliverance or prosperity or miracles, signs, wonders, etc. Rather, God's glorious kingdom revival that this real remnant generation will usher into the earth will be all about King Jesus and all He has in His kingdom for His people which includes everything I just mentioned and so much more.

Now, if you are not young in age, like me who is age 45 at the writing of this book, then do not worry. God is not leaving us out of His real remnant of revivalists. Although I have intentionally dedicated the majority of this chapter to expressing the great importance of the young generation being a major part of the real remnant of revivalists, I would also like to point out how the older generation was also included in the real remnant. How so? The answer is found in remembering that included in the 120 disciples, who were a real remnant that went to the upper room, were older adults such as Mary, the biological mother of Jesus. According to Bible scholars, during the time of Acts 1 and 2, she would have been approximately 46 to 50 years of age, since it is believed by many theologians that Mary was a teenager when she gave birth to Jesus Christ 33 years before the book of Acts.

Hence, there is room for people my age and older to be part of a modern-day upper room remnant for revival. Therefore, if you are in your 40s, 50s, or 60s, be encouraged to know we can all be part of the real revival remnant God is raising up in these last days. In fact, what matters most in God's kingdom, is not the actual number of our physical ages, but rather our actual hunger for more from our Lord of revival who is the King of the ages. Furthermore, when we consider the prophecy of Joel 2 and the apostolic fulfillment of Acts 2, we can recall that the outpouring of the Holy Spirit was promised to come upon all flesh of all ages, since children would prophesy, young people would see visions, and older people would dream dreams.

Therefore, this reminder should serve as a great encouragement for generations of all ages to become one spiritual generation that God can utilize as a real remnant of revivalists, regardless of age, gender, ethnicity, profession, social class, and any other human classification. In fact, I believe God will soon raise up a remnant of revivalists in every single sector of our national and international societies including those of government, military, education, business, medicine, athletics, entertainment, music, and much more. Together in Jesus Christ, we can be one spiritual generation of real remnant revivalists. Now, if you believe this with me, please join me in the next chapter, as we biblically and spiritually discover the revolutionary revelation of revival. History is in the making for the next great awakening, and I believe you and I are part of the real remnant for revival now!

CHAPTER 4
THE REVOLUTIONARY REVELATION

Have you heard about the revolutionary revelation of revival? This life-restoring and spirit-awakening scriptural insight is one I received from the Lord in my personal study of the Bible, when I was 18 years of age in San Antonio. God revealed it to me during one of the most spiritually intense seasons in my life of seeking His face, studying His word, and cultivating a profoundly intimate relationship with Jesus Christ and the Holy Spirit. It was during this season that I found myself spending hours on end with the Lord in the privacy of my bedroom, in addition to my parent's living room, early in the morning before they and my siblings would awaken.

Now before I share this revolutionary revelation of revival with you, it is of utmost importance I mention that the biblical basis for it is registered in Acts 2, and rooted in Joel 2, while also being supported by other scripture passages we will consider in this chapter. To begin with, let us consider two passages of scripture we looked at in the previous chapters of this book. Yet this time, we will see them from an additional perspective that has revolutionized my understanding of what occurred on the Day of Pentecost, through the outpouring of the Holy Spirit, and in connection to the revival which birthed the primitive church. Acts 2:16-17 and Joel 2:28 say:

> *[16] But this is what was spoken by the Prophet Joel:*
> *[17] "And it shall come to pass in the last days, says God,*
> *That I will pour out of My Spirit on all flesh;*
> *Your sons and your daughters shall prophesy,*
> *Your young men shall see visions,*
> *Your old men shall dream dreams."*
>
> *Acts 2:16-17 NKJV*

> *[28] And it shall come to pass afterward*
> *That I will pour out My Spirit on all flesh;*
> *Your sons and your daughters shall prophesy,*
> *Your old men shall dream dreams,*
> *Your young men shall see visions.*
>
> *Joel 2:28 NKJV*

It was through these two passages of scripture that the Lord began to reveal to me the revolutionary revelation of revival. Consequently, the Lord showed me this revelation had to do with what the Prophet Joel, and the Apostle Peter, mentioned regarding three generations being engaged by God, as a result of the outpouring of His Holy Spirit on the Day of Pentecost. In both of these passages, the Lord began by showing me that children would prophesy, young people would see visions, and older people would dream dreams. However, the Lord additionally showed me that this revelation was not only about a generational blessing for humanity, but it was also about a gradual progression of God's blessing to and through humanity. The revival revelation the Lord revealed to me was and is that when God's Holy Spirit descends upon a place and a people, then God's sovereign sequence and faith filled formula for His great moves to fulfill His promise and provide His salvation to all humanity occurs. So what is that sovereign sequence and faith-filled formula? 1) prophecies, 2) visions, and 3) dreams, result in and release God's providential reality.

Another way of viewing this sovereign sequence and faith-filled formula is by realizing that in God's kingdom, His word is first spoken, which is called prophecy. Second, His word is then seen, which is called a vision. Third, His word is eventually seeded or sown, which is called a dream. And His intended result is for His divinely spoken, seen, and sown word to eventually be birthed into our earthly existence in His heavenly time for us, which is our reality. Consequently, I believe that is one of the main reasons why Peter, in Acts 2:16-17, declared on the Day of Pentecost that children would prophesy, young people would see visions, and older people would dream dreams, so that ultimately everyone who calls upon the name of the Lord would be divinely saved.

Interestingly enough, this pattern of hearing, seeing, carrying, and then birthing the promise of God is also found at the beginning of Acts 2:1-6. Let us consider this passage from an additional perspective to what we considered in the previous chapters.

> *[1] When the Day of Pentecost had fully come, they were all with one accord in one place. [2] And suddenly there came a sound from heaven, as of a rushing mighty wind, and it filled the whole house where they were sitting. [3] Then there appeared to them divided tongues, as of fire, and one sat upon each of them. [4] And they were all filled with the Holy Spirit and began to speak with other tongues, as the Spirit gave them utterance. [5] And there were dwelling in Jerusalem Jews, devout men, from every nation under heaven. [6] And when this sound occurred, the multitude came together, and were confused, because everyone heard them speak in his own language.*
>
> *Acts 2:1-6 NKJV*

When we carefully consider this passage of scripture, we can observe that the 120 disciples in the upper room experienced three supernatural things. First, they heard a sound from heaven. Second, they saw flames of fire. Third, they were all filled with the Holy Spirit, and the ultimate end result to this sovereign sequence and faith-filled formula was the salvation of 3,000 souls which marked the birth of the Church. Yet what I find to be more intriguing than this particular observation in Acts 2:1-6, is the biblical fact, that this revolutionary revelation of revival was already rooted in the book of Genesis and reiterated in the book of Luke, long before the outpouring of the Holy Spirit occurred in Acts 2. Allow me to explain this through God's word and my corresponding observations. Consider Genesis 1:1-5, 11 which says:

> [1] *In the beginning God created the heavens and the earth.*
> [2] *The earth was without form, and void; and darkness was on the face of the deep. And the Spirit of God was hovering over the face of the waters.* [3] *Then God said, "Let there be light"; and there was light.* [4] *And God saw the light, that it was good; and God divided the light from the darkness.* [5] *God called the light Day, and the darkness He called Night. So the evening and the morning were the first day.*
>
> [11] *Then God said, "Let the earth bring forth grass, the herb that yields seed, and the fruit tree that yields fruit according to its kind, whose seed is in itself, on the earth"; and it was so.*
>
> *Genesis 1:1-5; 11 NKJV*

In Genesis 1, we can observe the following, which in principle is paralleled in Acts 2. First, God's Holy Spirit comes on the scene. Second, God prophetically speaks. Third, God creates a visible sight. Fourth, God sows a seed, and fifth, God brings forth a greater physical reality that began with a spiritual move of His Spirit. In principle, this revolutionary revelation also takes place in the lives of two couples in the Bible.

Consider the example of the Old Testament couple, Abraham and Sarah, in Genesis 15:1-6, and the complementing example of the New Testament couple, Joseph and Mary, in Luke 1:26-38.

> [1] *After these things the word of the LORD came to Abram in a vision, saying, "Do not be afraid, Abram. I am your shield, your exceedingly great reward."*
> [2] *But Abram said, "Lord GOD, what will You give me, seeing I go childless, and the heir of my house is Eliezer of Damascus?"* [3] *Then Abram said, "Look, You have given me no offspring; indeed one born in my house is my heir!"*
> [4] *And behold, the word of the LORD came to him, saying, "This one shall not be your heir, but one who will come from your own body shall be your heir."* [5] *Then He brought him outside and said, "Look now toward heaven, and count the stars if you are able to number them." And He said to him, "So shall your descendants be."*
> [6] *And he believed in the LORD, and He accounted it to him for righteousness.*
>
> Genesis 15:1-6 NKJV

> [26] *Now in the sixth month the angel Gabriel was sent by God to a city of Galilee named Nazareth,* [27] *to a virgin betrothed to a man whose name was Joseph, of the house of David. The virgin's name was Mary.* [28] *And having come in, the angel said to her, "Rejoice, highly favored one, the Lord is with you; blessed are you among women!"*
> [29] *But when she saw him, she was troubled at his saying, and considered what manner of greeting this was.* [30] *Then the angel said to her, "Do not be afraid, Mary, for you have found favor with God.* [31] *And behold, you will conceive in your womb and bring forth a Son, and shall call His name JESUS.* [32] *He will be great, and will be called the Son of the Highest; and the Lord God will give Him the throne of His*

father David. ^{33} And He will reign over the house of Jacob
forever, and of His kingdom there will be no end."
^{34} Then Mary said to the angel, "How can this be, since I do
not know a man?"
^{35} And the angel answered and said to her, "The Holy Spirit
will come upon you, and the power of the Highest will
overshadow you; therefore, also, that Holy One who is to be
born will be called the Son of God. ^{36} Now indeed, Elizabeth
your relative has also conceived a son in her old age; and
this is now the sixth month for her who was called barren.
^{37} For with God nothing will be impossible."
^{38} Then Mary said, "Behold the maidservant of the Lord!
Let it be to me according to your word." And the angel
departed from her.

Luke 1:26-38 NKJV

Intriguingly enough, in both instances, God or His angel
encountered one of the members of these couples with a type of
prophecy, a type of vision, and a type of dream, ultimately resulting in a
birthed reality of heaven on earth. The first instance resulted in the birth
of Isaac and the second instance resulted in the birth of Jesus. How did
this happen for both couples? Consider carefully what happened.
Abraham received God's foretelling word, also known as prophecy, that
he would have a son of promise and eventually promised descendants.
Abraham was then told by God to look at, also known as seeing a vision
of, the stars and the sand of the sea to see how his promised descendants
would be. Abraham and Sarah, thereafter, were supernaturally enabled
by God to conceive their child of promise, also known as receiving the
seed of their dream. Then, Abraham and Sarah carried their son of
promise in Sarah's womb until it was time for her to give birth to their
promised son, who was their promised reality.

On the other hand, Mary received God's word, also known as
prophecy, through the Angel Gabriel during a vision she had within a
dream. Mary received the prophecy, vision, and dream all at the same

time. On a very important side note, it is worth mentioning that sometimes God will accelerate His process, due to divinely set times for subsequent events that need to take place in His preappointed times. Either way, in many cases, God has to wait on humanity, instead of humanity waiting on Him. Returning to the text in Luke 1, Mary and Joseph eventually understood that the prophecy, visions, and dreams, including the additional four dreams Joseph received about Jesus registered in Matthew 1:18-25 and 2:1-23, were all part of God's process to bring the promised Messiah and Christ into the world in order to save the world. This was and still is God's intended reality promised to everyone who calls on Jesus as their Lord.

Now when I consider all of this as God's sovereign sequence and faith-filled formula for His people from Bible times to our post-modern times, I am truly amazed by this revolutionary revelation of revival. As a result, this then leads me to ask, "Now what about you and me?" What prophecies, visions, and dreams has God given us that need to be birthed through us, in order to fulfill His promise to us and to those connected to us? Subsequently, we should ask ourselves if we are prophetically speaking, envisioning, and dreaming that particular word of God which can release His promised life-giving revival? Or are we pathetically speaking, envisioning, and dreaming, in the form of a diabolic nightmare, the word of the enemy which will result in death?

When we consider this, I believe it can help us see Proverbs 18:21, James 3:5-6, and Acts 2:1-4 from an additional perspective we may have not considered before, as it pertains to the importance of what we use our mouths to speak.

21 Death and life are in the power of the tongue,
And those who love it will eat its fruit.

Proverbs 18:21 NKJV

5 Even so the tongue is a little member and boasts great things. See how great a forest a little fire kindles! 6 And the tongue is a fire, a world of iniquity. The tongue is so set

75

*among our members that it defiles the whole body, and sets
on fire the course of nature; and it is set on fire by hell.*

James 3:5-6 NKJV

*[1] When the Day of Pentecost had fully come, they were all
with one accord in one place. [2] And suddenly there came a
sound from heaven, as of a rushing mighty wind, and it
filled the whole house where they were sitting. [3] Then there
appeared to them divided tongues, as of fire, and one sat
upon each of them. [4] And they were all filled with the Holy
Spirit and began to speak with other tongues, as the Spirit
gave them utterance.*

Acts 2:1-4 NKJV

From the perspective of fully understanding the power of our
spoken words for our lives and the lives of others, these passages of
scripture can jointly help us realize two profound truths. The first is
realizing how extremely important and influential our words are. The
second is understanding that one of the main reasons why the 120
disciples on the Day of Pentecost began to speak in tongues was to
prophetically declare the wonders of God in other languages which
captivated the attention of 3,000 people who would soon get saved.

Next, we should ask ourselves, are we seeing the vision God has
shown or desires to show us? With that question in mind, let us
remember how profoundly vital a vision is for our lives according to
Proverbs 29:18 and Habakkuk 2:2-3 which says:

*[18] Where there is no vision, the people perish: but he that
keepeth the law, happy is he.*

Proverbs 29:18 KJV

*[2] Then the LORD answered me and said:
"Write the vision
And make it plain on tablets,*

76

That he may run who reads it.
³ For the vision is yet for an appointed time;
But at the end it will speak, and it will not lie.
Though it tarries, wait for it;
Because it will surely come,
It will not tarry.

Habakkuk 2:2-3 NKJV

From the concept of completely comprehending how vital a vision is for our lives and the lives of others, these scripture passages together help us recognize two additional profound truths. The first is understanding how deeply essential and influential it is to have a divine vision for our lives. The second is understanding that one of the main reasons why the 120 disciples on the Day of Pentecost experienced the visible sign of tongues of fire coming upon their heads was to cause thousands of other people to desire the holy fire that was burning in their lives.

Continuing on, we should ask ourselves, are we carrying the dream God has sown into us? With that question in mind, let us remember how extremely important and influential God-given dreams are according to Numbers 12:6 and Matthew 1:20, 2:13, 2:19, 2:22 which say:

⁶ Then He said,
"Hear now My words:
If there is a prophet among you,
I, the LORD, make Myself known to him in a vision;
I speak to him in a dream."

Numbers 12:6 NKJV

²⁰ But while he thought about these things, behold, an angel
of the Lord appeared to him in a dream, saying, "Joseph,
son of David, do not be afraid to take to you Mary your

77

wife, for that which is conceived in her is of the Holy Spirit."

Matthew 1:20 NKJV

[13] Now when they had departed, behold, an angel of the Lord appeared to Joseph in a dream, saying, "Arise, take the young Child and His mother, flee to Egypt, and stay there until I bring you word; for Herod will seek the young Child to destroy Him."

[19] Now when Herod was dead, behold, an angel of the Lord appeared in a dream to Joseph in Egypt,

[22] But when he heard that Archelaus was reigning over Judea instead of his father Herod, he was afraid to go there. And being warned by God in a dream, he turned aside into the region of Galilee.

Matthew 2:13; 2:19; 2:22 NKJV

From the perspective of completely acknowledging how life-changing divine dreams are for our lives and the lives of others, these scripture passages jointly help us recognize yet two more profound truths. The first is understanding how extensively paramount and purposeful it is to have a divine dream for our lives. The second is understanding that one of the main reasons why the 120 disciples on the Day of Pentecost were filled with the Holy Spirit was so they could help lead 3,000 other people towards salvation in Christ.

Now considering all of that, this revolutionary revelation of revival is truly powerful. Prophecies, visions, and dreams, ultimately should result in a divine reality for our lives and the lives of many others around us. Therefore, I believe that it is time for the revolutionary revelation of revival to come to us, be conceived in us, be carried by us, so it can then be birthed through us. With that in mind, and in order for us to fully understand why we must have revival, please join me in the next chapter to discover the relevant reasons for revival now. History is in the making for the next great awakening, and the revolutionary revelation of revival in our lives has the potential of resulting in us birthing the next great move of God!

CHAPTER 5
THE RELEVANT REASONS

In our post-modern era in which being relevant is of extreme importance to all generations of our multiethnic, multicultural, and multifaceted national and international societies, I believe there is a great question worth asking, as it pertains to revival. Is having revival now relevant for our nation and the nations of the world?

Amid the current COVID-19 growing global pandemic and the increasingly rising racial tensions in our nation, I believe there is a great and grave answer to this question. In fact, I say this due to the first part of the definition of revival being "restoration to life," as we discovered in the second chapter of this book. When we consider how much loss of life, health, wealth, racial unity, and so much more our world, and especially our country, have experienced in just the first half of this year, I am wholeheartedly convinced having revival now is extremely relevant for our present times. In fact, having revival now is perhaps more relevant now, than ever before.

Additionally, I also say there is a great and grave answer to this question of revival relevancy, based on my personal experiences as a 45-year old Puerto Rican U.S. Citizen born in Rochester, New York, who has lived in New York, Texas, California, and Pennsylvania throughout my lifetime, with the majority of my years having been lived in San Antonio and now in the Dallas County Area where I gladly live in a predominantly Black community I love. In fact, it is worth mentioning, based on my DNA test results, that God has blessed me with a multi-ethnic genetic make-up connected to Puerto Rico, Portugal, Spain, Cameroon, Congo, Senegal, Nigeria, Northern Africa, Ireland, Scotland, and France, in addition to having a connection to European Jews.

Correspondingly, I also say there is a great and grave answer to this question, based on my experiences of being married to Mildred for 24 years now, having our three children Gabriella, Samantha, and David, who are currently ages 23, 21, and 19, and having served in denominational and non-denominational multiethnic bilingual ministry for 23 years in various ministerial capacities including those of evangelistic, pastoral, and Christian education ministry, in addition to pro-Israel advocacy. However, please know I do not mention all of this as an egotistic attempt to share an impressive resume, but rather as an experienced individual to show the informed and experiential relevance from which I will draw to share with you in this chapter.

Yet moreover, and far more importantly, I believe the great and grave answer to the question at hand, is in much greater part, based on the exegesis and exposition of God's eternal word and this timeless message for all humanity throughout our nation and around the world in times past, present, and future. With that in mind, I dare say that the most relevant book and message for all humanity on planet Earth is the Bible and its Good News message, not the news of any particular television network, physical or electronic newspaper, social media platform or additional sources of modern messaging. The unfortunate reality is that many of these outlets are attempting to question the very existence and omniscience of our eternal and all-knowing God who all by Himself created humanity in His own image and likeness without requiring anyone's permission.

Now when I combine our world and nation's post-modern era pandemic problems, together with my personal and ministerial experiences and the Bible's exegesis and exposition on the question of revival relevancy, I consider what I believe to be the five most relevant reasons for revival now. Of course, there are additional reasons, but unfortunately, I do not have the time nor the space to cover them in this chapter. Consequently, I will focus on the five most relevant reasons. So what are they, and what can we learn from them? To begin with, I will list them and then go through each of them one by one.

- Relevant Reason #1: Our salvation and the salvation of others depend on it right now.
- Relevant Reason #2: God has revived His people before and He can do it again.
- Relevant Reason #3: We have arrived to a moment of mercy.
- Relevant Reason #4: We have a window of opportunity.
- Relevant Reason #5: History is in the making for the next great awakening.

Let us consider the first relevant reason for revival: "Our salvation and the salvation of others depends on it right now." I believe this reason to be so, based on God's word in Romans 13:11 which says:

> *[11] And do this, knowing the time, that now it is high time to awake out of sleep; for now our salvation is nearer than when we first believed.*
>
> *Romans 13:11 NKJV*

In this passage, the Apostle Paul reveals to us we must recognize the high time to awaken out of a spiritual state of being asleep because our salvation and the salvation of others is nearer than what we might think. Additionally, the Apostle Paul reiterates, in another letter he wrote, the importance of us realizing that now is the time for us and for others to receive God's salvation, according to 2 Corinthians 6:1-2 which says:

*[1] We then, as workers together with Him also plead with you
not to receive the grace of God in vain. [2] For He says:
"In an acceptable time I have heard you,
And in the day of salvation I have helped you."
Behold, now is the accepted time; behold, now is the day of
salvation.*

2 Corinthians 6:1-2

To better understand now is the time for our salvation, including those of our loved ones who have not yet been saved, we should reflect on four children's ministry and youth-young adult ministry staggering statistics produced by the very reputable and highly respected Barna Research Group (TBG) and the widely-renowned Life Way Research (LWR) organization. Mildred and I first began to hear about the first three of these four staggering statistics during the time we served as the High School Youth Ministry and College and Career Young Adult Pastors for Cornerstone Church in San Antonio, Texas from 2008 through 2013. Subsequently, the fourth statistic, I found out about, after my time on pastoral staff at Cornerstone Church, as an evangelist with a passion for revival now. So what are these four staggering statistics?

- 1st staggering statistic by TBG in 2003: American children ages of 5 to 13 have a 32% probability of becoming Christians.[1]

- 2nd staggering statistic by TBG in 2003: American youth ages 14 to 18 have a 4% probability of becoming Christians.[1]

- 3rd staggering statistic by TBG in 2003: American young adults age 19 and over have just a 6% probability of becoming Christians.[1]

- 4th staggering statistic by LWR in 2017: 66% of youth, who attended church services at least twice a month for at least one year during their teen years, ended up leaving the Church during the ages of 18 to 22.[2]

Now when we consider all of these relevant and staggering statistics, I believe they provide great and grave cause for us to spiritually wake up for revival now. Truth be told, they are outright alarming. The undeniable fact is that we are presently living in a post-modern era in which there is a great urgency for a "resurgence" or revival. Resurgence is another way of saying revival, and by definition, it root word of "resurge" literally means "rising or tending to rise again; reviving; renascent; to rise again, as from desuetude or from virtual extinction; to rise again, appear again." Its word origin is as follows:

"equiv. To re- RE- + surgere to lift up, raise, var. Of surrigere (sur- SUR-2 + -rigere, comb. Form ofregere to direct, rule)]."[3]

Considering this definition and word origin for resurge, I profoundly believe God desires to revive the next generation now so they can rise up, rule, and direct or influence their peers and younger generation to do the same. In fact, I must say that in my personal, parental, and ministerial experiences and observations, the young generations are not just the "Next Gen," as some understandably call them. While I do agree that they are the next generation of all kinds of professionals and influencers in our nation and beyond, at the same time, I wholeheartedly believe they are also the "generation now" that has far more influence on their peers than we adults will ever have on them. Additionally, I would also dare to say that the level of influence they have on the younger children, who highly esteem them, is either comparable or even greater than the influence of some adults. Therefore, so goes the "next generation," so goes the following generation that is following after them. Therefore, we must have revival now, because our salvation and the salvation of the younger generations depend on it at this present moment in time.

Moving onto the second relevant reason for revival now, let us consider that "God has revived His people before and He can do it again." This reason is biblically based on Habakkuk 3:1-5 which says:

¹ A prayer of Habakkuk the prophet. On shigionoth.
² LORD, I have heard of your fame;
   I stand in awe of your deeds, LORD.
Repeat them in our day,
   in our time make them known;
   in wrath remember mercy.
³ God came from Teman,
   the Holy One from Mount Paran.
His glory covered the heavens
   and his praise filled the earth.
⁴ His splendor was like the sunrise;
   rays flashed from his hand,
   where his power was hidden.
⁵ Plague went before him;
   pestilence followed his steps.

Habakkuk 3:1-5 NIV

What an interesting passage of Old Testament prophetic scripture I believe can connect to our 2020 COVID-19 global pandemic times. It is worth noting that the prophet Habakkuk lived during a time in which his nation of Israel was not obeying their God of Israel as they should have. Consequently, one of their enemy nations, Assyria, took advantage of their disobedience and attacked them. During that time, Habakkuk did at least three things that are registered in the scripture passage we just read. The first thing he did was to pray to God. The second thing he did was to let God know he had heard of God's past powerful works. The third thing he did was ask God to revive His work in the midst of the years, solely based on His mercy. As a result, God responded with His glory and power, and interestingly enough, a plague went before God and a pestilence followed God's footsteps. Then in the rest of Habakkuk 3, God judged the enemy King of Assyria who had come against Habakkuk's nation, Israel.

Now over 2,600 years later in 2020, I am compelled to ask a question. Can the same be said about our nation of the United States of America, as well as of an enemy nation, and the plague or pestilence that has crippled our nation and the nations of the world? Perhaps, God is revealing to us that He wants our nation to return to Him. Perhaps, God desires for His ministers in our nation to pray to Him for revival now. Perhaps, God is longing for our nation to look to Him to respond with His great glory and power in the midst of the current plague. Perhaps, God does plan on dealing with the enemies that have come against our nation. Perhaps, God could very well be releasing a prophetic message to our nation and the Body of Jesus Christ within it. Therefore, now more than ever, we must understand God has revived other generations in times past, and He can mercifully do it again in our present times, especially in our nation that needs another great awakening.

Consider, in general view, our nation's prior Great Awakenings or revivals that occurred in the 1700s, 1800s, and 1900s. These Great Awakenings spiritually awakened the Church, reached the lost, influenced society, reformed government, impacted educational institutions, promoted racial reconciliation, and contributed greatly to the greatness of our nation. Although the aim of this section is not to deeply dive into each of the revivals that have happened in our nation since the 1700s, I will point out, interestingly enough, that the first Great Awakening in our nation is said to have started in its inception, approximately 300 years ago, in the 1720s. The undercurrent of the first great wave of revival to come to our nation's shores in the 1700s began with a German American Dutch Reformed minister and theologian by the name of Theodorus Jacobus Frelinghuysen, and it occurred in the Raritan Valley of New Jersey. Now when I consider the timing of the beginning of the undercurrent for the first spiritual wave of revival and Great Awakening in our nation to have happened in the 20s of a past century, I do not believe that to be happenstance. Neither do I believe it to be a coincidence, considering the fact that we are now in the 20s of our present century. On the contrary, I perceive it to be a God-incident in which He is gracefully and mercifully inciting us to pursue Him for revival in our present time, because He has been faithful to revive our nation in past times. Gleaning from the 1720s, it was then that minister Theodorus Frelinghuysen, like the prophet Habakkuk, prayed for God to revive His powerful work in the midst of the years, and God did it. Now what if you and I were to pray like Frelinghuysen and Habakkuk? What if you and I were to believe that because God revived our nation back then, then surely He can revive it again? I believe God is well able to do it, and I believe He will do it because of His great mercy for us. All we have to do is follow suit in the example of Habakkuk. God has revived His people before, and He can do it again.

Let us move onto the third relevant reason for revival now, and consider that "we have arrived to a moment of mercy." This reason is biblically based on Psalm 85:4-7 which says:

> *⁴ Restore us, O God of our salvation,*
> *And cause Your anger toward us to cease.*
> *⁵ Will You be angry with us forever?*
> *Will You prolong Your anger to all generations?*
> *⁶ Will You not revive us again,*
> *That Your people may rejoice in You?*
> *⁷ Show us Your mercy, LORD,*
> *And grant us Your salvation.*
>
> *Psalm 85:4-7 NKJV*

In this passage, the psalmist is either a son or descendant of Korah. Interestingly enough, it is worth noting Korah, in Numbers 16, rebelled against Moses and was consequently killed by God because of his rebellion. Correspondingly, one of his descendants learns a hard lesson from Korah's rebellion, and in Psalm 85 begins to recall how God in times past had: 1) shown His favor to His people, 2) restored their fortunes, 3) forgiven their iniquities, 4) covered their sins, 5) set aside His wrath, and 6) turned away from His fierce anger against His people who were not living right before Him. Why was he making this observation? Because as a descendant of Korah, there is great probability he was either referring to his first-hand eyewitness of, or the stories passed down the generational lines of, Korah and God's sovereign shift from a justifiable righteous wrath to a gracious expression of mercy to His people. Therefore, the psalmist asks God: 1) to restore them again, 2) to not be angry with His people any longer, and 3) to revive them instead, so they can once again rejoice in Him and receive His love and salvation.

Yet why would the psalmist approach God in this way? I believe it is because in addition to having personally seen or heard about how God had revived His people in the past, the psalmist understood that from time to time, humanity arrives to moments of mercy during which we must cry out to God for mercy. When I consider how our God has been so good to our nation in the past, but we have still managed to stray from Him and disobey His word in various ways such as idolatry, immorality, infidelity, abortion, extortion, corruption, racism, and so much more going on in our nation to this very day, I understand a very sobering, yet encouraging, truth for our sinfully intoxicated United States. This merciful truth is that although God has the right to judge us and our nation, instead of Him doing so and due to His great favor, forgiveness, and desire to restore us, we can approach His throne of grace and cry out for mercy today. Consequently, that is what we must do in this year and onward, because I believe we have arrived to another moment of mercy.

Therefore, now more than ever, we must cry out to God for mercy in the moment we are now in. When I think about doing so and consider a biblical example of such a cry for mercy going forth, I am reminded of a man named Bartimaeus who was in great and grave need of mercy according to Mark 10:46-52 which says:

> *⁴⁶ Now they came to Jericho. As He went out of Jericho with His disciples and a great multitude, blind Bartimaeus, the son of Timaeus, sat by the road begging. ⁴⁷ And when he*

*heard that it was Jesus of Nazareth, he began to cry out and
say, "Jesus, Son of David, have mercy on me!"*
*⁴⁸ Then many warned him to be quiet; but he cried out all
the more, "Son of David, have mercy on me!"*
*⁴⁹ So Jesus stood still and commanded him to be called.
Then they called the blind man, saying to him, "Be of good
cheer. Rise, He is calling you."*
*⁵⁰ And throwing aside his garment, he rose and came to
Jesus.*
*⁵¹ So Jesus answered and said to him, "What do you want
Me to do for you?"*
*The blind man said to Him, "Rabboni, that I may receive
my sight."*
*⁵² Then Jesus said to him, "Go your way; your faith has
made you well." And immediately he received his sight and
followed Jesus on the road.*

Mark 10:46-52 NKJV

In this passage of scripture, we see that Bartimaeus' encounter
with Jesus Christ was not necessarily on Jesus' original ministry
itinerary. But regardless, Bartimaeus cried out to Jesus for the restoration
of his sight, which was in itself a form of revival by definition,
considering that revival is restoration to life. In this case, Bartimaeus
needed to receive the restoration of his sight. Although Bartimaeus was
told by Jesus' disciples to be quiet, he cried out to Jesus all the more for
mercy. Therefore, because of his continual cry for mercy, Jesus stopped
and eventually restored his sight.

Now in 2020, which many leaders throughout our nation and
around the world have understandably called "the year of 20/20 vision"
or something to that effect, I believe we have arrived to a moment of
mercy during which we can cry out to Jesus to restore our spiritual sight
or vision, especially when we consider how the COVID-19 growing
global pandemic and increasingly rising racial tensions in our nation
have blinded, to a certain extent, the foresight of our nation and the

nations of the world. The reality is that the current global pandemic and national racial tensions have blinded the vision of so many leaders and groups of people in our nation in an unprecedented and unparalleled way. To the point that, we as a nation, together with nations around the world, are struggling to clearly see what our future will actually be like in the upcoming months, year, and perhaps even beyond that.

Therefore, we must become like Bartimaeus and cry out all the more to our Lord for mercy, even though we do not deserve it according to Isaiah 64:6 which says:

> *⁶ But we are all like an unclean thing,*
> *And all our righteousnesses are like filthy rags;*
> *We all fade as a leaf,*
> *And our iniquities, like the wind,*
> *Have taken us away.*
>
> *Isaiah 64:6 NKJV*

In this scripture, we can spiritually see that although our human righteousness does not deserve to have our vision restored or revived by Jesus Christ, He does deserve to have our vision for Him restored and revived, so we can seek Him clearly, as we should. All we have to do is humble ourselves before Him who is the High and Lofty One, and He will revive us according to Isaiah 57:15 which says:

> *¹⁵ For thus says the High and Lofty One*
> *Who inhabits eternity, whose name is Holy:*
> *"I dwell in the high and holy place,*
> *With him who has a contrite and humble spirit,*
> *To revive the spirit of the humble,*
> *And to revive the heart of the contrite ones."*
>
> *Isaiah 57:15 NKJV*

Yes, our God of revival desires to revive us as we seek Him in humility, because as I said before, I wholeheartedly believe we have arrived to a moment of mercy.

Moving onto the fourth relevant reason for revival now, let us consider that "we have a window of opportunity." This reason is biblically based on Ezra 9:8-9 which says:

> [8] *And now for a little while grace has been shown from the LORD our God, to leave us a remnant to escape, and to give us a peg in His holy place, that our God may enlighten our eyes and give us a measure of revival in our bondage. [9] For we were slaves. Yet our God did not forsake us in our bondage; but He extended mercy to us in the sight of the kings of Persia, to revive us, to repair the house of our God, to rebuild its ruins, and to give us a wall in Judah and Jerusalem.*
>
> *Ezra 9:8-9 NKJV*

In this passage, Ezra the priest reveals through his prayer that there is a window of opportunity for revival. In his case, the people of Israel had recently returned, from being exiled in Babylon, to Jerusalem where the restoration of the people of Israel, the city of Jerusalem, and the temple were underway. As a result, Ezra makes it clear that there was: 1) a limited time of grace and mercy available, 2) a remnant who God had spared, 3) an enlightenment of the eyes so His people could see clearly, and 4) a measure of revival in the midst of their bondage. All of this was done to collectively serve for the purpose of God's people refocusing their attention on rebuilding God's temple, the city of Jerusalem, and the people of Israel.

Now in this 2020 year, which numerically can represent 20/20 vision and therefore be connected to the importance of eyesight or enlightenment, considering the major negative effects of COVID-19 and the rising racial tensions on the lives, health, and wealth of our nation and beyond, I believe God is telling us through His word that we have

92

received a window of opportunity. This opportunity is one of His great grace and mercy so we, as His remnant, can regain our spiritual vision and see there is indeed a measure of revival now available to us. I believe this to be the case, even amid the recent bondage we experienced earlier this year by the shelter in place orders issued throughout our nation and around the world.

Just as it was in Ezra's time for him and God's remnant people to see and seize the gracious and merciful window of opportunity God was presenting them, I believe we can seize the same gracious and merciful window of opportunity God is making available to us. Subsequently, when we do, then we will be able to return to Him, focus on rebuilding His spiritual house in our nation, and secure our spiritual borders so the attack of past and even future enemies will not be able to successfully attack us again in the days ahead. Therefore, we must seize the current window of opportunity for revival now.

Otherwise, if we do not take advantage of it, then we might just as well lose it, because we may very well be living in a "now or never" moment. One of the greatest examples of this kind of moment is registered in Luke 19, when some 500 plus years after Ezra is in Jerusalem, Jesus Christ comes into the same city, surrounded by the similar walls, with a similar temple and people in general. Consider Luke 19:41-44 which says:

[41] Now as He drew near, He saw the city and wept over it, [42] saying, "If you had known, even you, especially in this your day, the things that make for your peace! But now they are hidden from your eyes. [43] For days will come upon you when your enemies will build an embankment around you, surround you and close you in on every side, [44] and level you, and your children within you, to the ground; and they will not leave in you one stone upon another, because you did not know the time of your visitation."

Luke 19:41-44 NKJV

In this passage of scripture, unfortunately, we see that because many of the Jews of that time in Jerusalem did not recognize their gracious and merciful great window of opportunity, there were grave consequences which negatively affected the Jewish people, the land of Israel, the city of Jerusalem, the temple of God, and more. Therefore, we must learn from both Ezra's and Jesus' times and seize this window of opportunity for revival now. In fact, I believe we must seek God for a gracious and merciful divine visitation, and expect to receive it from Him. When we do, not only will He faithfully grant it to us, but I believe He will also gloriously gift us with a divine habitation of His glory and power according to Revelation 3:20-21 which says:

> *[20] Behold, I stand at the door and knock. If anyone hears My voice and opens the door, I will come in to him and dine with him, and he with Me. [21] To him who overcomes I will grant to sit with Me on My throne, as I also overcame and sat down with My Father on His throne.*
>
> *Revelation 3:20-21 NKJV*

Here we see that Jesus Christ gives His people the wonderfully glorious hope that not only can we recognize the window of opportunity He is presenting to us which can result in a divine visitation from Him. But even greater than that, we can proceed from experiencing a divine visitation to abiding in a divine habitation with Him in His glorious presence. Therefore, now more than ever, we must realize there is a window of opportunity.

Last, but certainly not least, let us move onto the fifth and final relevant reason for revival now, and consider that "history is in the making for the next great awakening." The biblical bases for this reason is in Ephesians 5:14 and Acts 17:26-27 in which the Apostle Paul says the following to the Church in Ephesus and then to the people in Athens:

> *[14] Therefore He says:*

"Awake, you who sleep,
Arise from the dead,
And Christ will give you light."

Ephesians 5:14 NKJV

[26] *From one man he made all the nations, that they should*
inhabit the whole earth; and he marked out their appointed
times in history and the boundaries of their lands. [27] *God*
did this so that they would seek him and perhaps reach out
for him and find him, though he is not far from any one of
us.

Acts 17:26-27 NIV

In these scripture passages, the Apostle Paul reveals in Ephesians 5:14 that during a time in which the Christians in Ephesus were surrounded by so much spiritual darkness, which included idolatry, immorality, impurity, covetousness, perversion, corrupt character, and other major issues of sin, the believers needed to spiritually wake up, rise up, and light up in order to overcome the darkness around them with the light of Jesus Christ upon them. Only by doing so could history be in the making for the next great awakening of their time. Additionally, in Acts 17:26-27, the Apostle Paul tells the agnostics in Athens that the unknown God to whom they had built an altar of worship was indeed his God and Lord Jesus Christ. Paul further tells them that it was his God who had created all of humanity and the nations of the earth, throughout world history, with the hope that they would seek Him and find Him.

Now when I consider 2020 and our nation, along with the nations of the world, unfortunately on one hand, I have to painfully admit that today we are facing similar times filled with so much of the same spiritual darkness that severely requires for the Church to spiritually wake up, rise up, and light up. Additionally, when I consider the growing number of agnostics throughout our nation and around the world, I have to contritely confess that in our present times we are dealing with an era filled with so much of the same idolatrous worship of the unknown which gravely demands for the Body of Christ to awaken, arise, and alight in Christ. Yet on the other hand, I prophetically proclaim and apostolically announce, with the deepest of biblical and spiritual convictions, that history is in the making for the next Great Awakening in our time. This divine declaration is not only for this year, but also for this next decade.

In fact, I am believing, praying, and expecting to see over the next decade, a great awakening, a great uprising, and a great enlightenment of the kind that only God and Jesus Christ can provide. Therefore, I declare a global great awakening, because we Christians need to wake up out of our spiritual sleep and comatose state. I declare a global great uprising, because we Christians need to rise up against the kingdom of darkness and all of its evil schemes; and I declare a global great enlightenment, because we Christians need to influence educational institutions with the kingdom principles of God's Word and with the knowledge of the glory of the Lord. This three-fold divine declaration I dare to humanly declare, because of the deep biblical conviction I spiritually sense from our great God, our Lord Jesus Christ, His Holy Spirit, and the authority of His word.

In fact, I wholeheartedly believe we are in a prophetic, apostolic, and divine day for the Body of Christ in which history will be made by the Christ of His body. Allow me to explain. Just as Ephesians 5:14 reveals the great importance for believers to wake up, rise up, and light up, there is a complementing clarion call in the Old Testament prophetic scripture of Hosea 6:2 which says:

> *² After two days He will revive us;*
> *On the third day He will raise us up,*
> *That we may live in His sight.*
>
> Hosea 6:2 NKJV

This Bible verse first became of huge importance to me in 1999 to 2000 when my former Pastor Samuel Rodriguez, Jr., began to preach a prophetically profound and powerful message series regarding "Third

Day Christians." He began preaching it in Staten Island, New York at Third Day Worship Center, where he was pastoring at the time. It was there where he had graced me with the great opportunity to serve as one of his Associate Pastors, Worship Pastor, and thereafter as his Co-Pastor. During that season of ministry, Pastor Rodriguez, also granted me the privilege of helping him type and slightly contribute to his book "Are You A Third Day Christian?" (published in 2000 by Creation House). Additionally, he also granted me the honor of traveling with him as his translator and worship leader throughout our nation, Puerto Rico, and Central America. Correspondingly, because of the great revelation God had revealed to Pastor Rodriguez about the third day for the Body of Christ, I was extremely blessed to glean from all the Lord was showing him, especially since I was his translator at the time. Some of the great insights I learned from this first-hand ministerial experience regarding the Body of Christ's third day was that in Hosea 6:2, the prophet revealed there would come a day in which God would revive, raise up, and cause His people to live in His sight.

Now although I fully understand this word first applies to God's prophetic promise to His beloved nation of Israel and to His cherished Jewish people, I also understand, that through the Jewish blood of His Only-Begotten Son, Jesus Christ, which has grafted us Gentile Christians into the spiritual olive tree God began with Abraham and continued with the Jewish people, it also applies to us who have believed in Jesus Christ by faith in the same way Abraham believed in God. Therefore, interestingly enough, this prophetic promise speaks of a certain day that applies to both Israel and to the Church. That day is the day after the second day, which is the third day.

With that in mind, in order for us to understand what that clearly means, it would help us to consider what the Apostle Peter said in 2 Peter 3:8 which says:

> [8] *But, beloved, do not forget this one thing, that with the Lord one day is as a thousand years, and a thousand years as one day.*

2 Peter 3:8 NKJV

According to this scripture, if one day to the Lord is as one thousand years and vice versa, then since the time of Jesus Christ's death, burial, and resurrection, the Body of Christ, has existed for approximately 2,000 years or two days. Additionally, since we began a new millennium 20 years ago, then the same collective Body of Christ is in its third millennium, also known as the third day. Now when we consider the many third day occurrences registered throughout the Bible, we can discover they were very historic and brought about great awakenings in their respective times.

Some examples, just to name a few, are:

- Abraham offering Isaac on the altar on the third day and God giving Isaac back to him on Mount Moriah,
- Esther going before King Xerxes on the third day and obtaining favor in his sight so she could deliver the Jewish people in Persia,
- Jonah being vomited out of the belly of the whale on the third day so he could administer repentance and revival to the entire city of Nineveh,
- Jesus' first earthly miracle being performed in which He changed water into wine on the third day in demonstration of His glory in Cana of Galilee,
- and the list goes on and on...

But the greatest third day occurrence, without a shadow of a doubt, was and will always be Jesus Christ Himself resurrecting from the dead and conquering Satan, sin, death, hell, and the grave, so He could offer eternal life to all of us, who would choose to be saved by calling upon His name, especially now in our present millennial third day.

Therefore, I truly believe we are in the greatest historic, prophetic, and apostolic day of revival that the Body of Christ has ever been in. In fact, I truly believe we will soon see history in the making for the next great awakening. Our third day is fully here, and it is time for us to be made alive with Christ, be raised up with Christ, and be seated with

Christ in heavenly places according to Ephesians 2:4-6 and Acts 17:28 which say:

> *⁴ But God, who is rich in mercy, because of His great love with which He loved us, ⁵ even when we were dead in trespasses, made us alive together with Christ (by grace you have been saved), ⁶ and raised us up together, and made us sit together in the heavenly places in Christ Jesus,*
> *Ephesians 2:4-6 NKJV*

> *²⁸ 'For in him we live and move and have our being.' As some of your own poets have said, 'We are his offspring.'*
> *Acts 17:28 NIV*

In these passages of scripture, we can fully understand that in this third day, the Body of Jesus Christ in our nation and throughout the world, lives in Christ, moves in Christ, and has its being in Christ. Therefore, may we collectively believe that history is in the making for the next great awakening, and may we never forget that what God is about to epically do on earth is not about any one man of God, ministry of God nor movement of God. Instead, it has been and always will be about the one Messiah sent from God, as clearly portrayed by Mark 9:1-8 which says:

> *¹ And He said to them, "Assuredly, I say to you that there are some standing here who will not taste death till they see the kingdom of God present with power."*
> *² Now after six days Jesus took Peter, James, and John, and led them up on a high mountain apart by themselves; and He was transfigured before them. ³ His clothes became shining, exceedingly white, like snow, such as no launderer on earth can whiten them. ⁴ And Elijah appeared to them with Moses, and they were talking with Jesus. ⁵ Then Peter answered and said to Jesus, "Rabbi, it is good for us to be*

here; and let us make three tabernacles: one for You, one for Moses, and one for Elijah"— ⁶ because he did not know what to say, for they were greatly afraid.
⁷ And a cloud came and overshadowed them; and a voice came out of the cloud, saying, "This is My beloved Son. Hear Him!" ⁸ Suddenly, when they had looked around, they saw no one anymore, but only Jesus with themselves.

Mark 9:1-8 NKJV

Here we see that just as it was in the New Testament times, during our present post-modern times, Jesus Christ must be the only One we lift up, so all humanity can be drawn to Him, just as He Himself declared it in John 12:32 which says:

³² And I, if I am lifted up from the earth, will draw all peoples to Myself.

John 12:32 NKJV

Therefore, let us exalt Jesus Christ above all and get ready to see all humanity that calls upon His name be saved, delivered, healed, and so much more, by God's grace and for His glory through faith in Christ.

Now that we have understood the five relevant reasons for revival now, I encourage you to keep reading this book and prepare to find out in the next chapter what we must do to position and posture ourselves in Christ so we can receive a personal Pentecost from Him. History is in the making for the next great awakening, and there is more than enough relevant reason for God to release revival now to us and through us to everyone around us!

CHAPTER 6
THE REVERENT RUDIMENTS

In 2010, one of the greatest lessons I learned in shifting from a season of depression into a season of revival, was the reality that simply desiring to have revival in my life was not enough. I needed to also deeply discover the realization that there are reverent rudiments for revival which God requires from a life that seeks to be revived. However, since the words reverent and rudiments are not words the average human being uses in his or her vernacular, you might be asking the following questions: "What does the phrase, 'reverent rudiments,' even mean?" "What are 'reverent rudiments' for revival according to the Bible?" "Why are they so important?" In order to answer these three questions, let us first consider God's word in Acts 1:1-8, 12-20, and Acts 2:1 which say:

> *¹ The former account I made, O Theophilus, of all that Jesus began both to do and teach, ² until the day in which He was taken up, after He through the Holy Spirit had given commandments to the apostles whom He had chosen, ³ to whom He also presented Himself alive after His suffering by*

*many infallible proofs, being seen by them during forty days
and speaking of the things pertaining to the kingdom of
God.*
*[4] And being assembled together with them, He commanded
them not to depart from Jerusalem, but to wait for the
Promise of the Father, "which," He said, "you have heard
from Me; [5] for John truly baptized with water, but you shall
be baptized with the Holy Spirit not many days from now."
[6] Therefore, when they had come together, they asked Him,
saying, "Lord, will You at this time restore the kingdom to
Israel?" [7] And He said to them, "It is not for you to know
times or seasons which the Father has put in His own
authority. [8] But you shall receive power when the Holy
Spirit has come upon you; and you shall be witnesses to Me
in Jerusalem, and in all Judea and Samaria, and to the end
of the earth."*

*[12] Then they returned to Jerusalem from the mount called
Olivet, which is near Jerusalem, a Sabbath day's journey.
[13] And when they had entered, they went up into the upper
room where they were staying: Peter, James, John, and
Andrew; Philip and Thomas; Bartholomew and Matthew;
James the son of Alphaeus and Simon the Zealot; and Judas
the son of James. [14] These all continued with one accord in
prayer and supplication, with the women and Mary the
mother of Jesus, and with His brothers.
[15] And in those days Peter stood up in the midst of the
disciples (altogether the number of names was about a
hundred and twenty), and said, [16] "Men and brethren, this
Scripture had to be fulfilled, which the Holy Spirit spoke
before by the mouth of David concerning Judas, who
became a guide to those who arrested Jesus; [17] for he was
numbered with us and obtained a part in this ministry."*

[18] (Now this man purchased a field with the wages of iniquity; and falling headlong, he burst open in the middle and all his entrails gushed out. [19] And it became known to all those dwelling in Jerusalem; so that field is called in their own language, Akel Dama, that is, Field of Blood.)
[20] "For it is written in the Book of Psalms:
'Let his dwelling place be desolate,
And let no one live in it';
and,
'Let another take his office.'

Acts 1:1-8, 12-20 NKJV

[1] When the Day of Pentecost had fully come, they were all with one accord in one place.

Acts 2:1 NKJV

In these passages of scripture, related to the revival that began in the upper room leading up to the Day of Pentecost and beyond, we can begin to discover the reverent rudiments for revival. However, before we specifically identify them, let us first consider the definitions of "reverent," "reverence," and "rudiment," in order to help us in our discovery of the reverent rudiments for revival:

- Reverent: feeling, exhibiting, or characterized by reverence; deeply respectful.
- Reverence: a feeling or attitude of deep respect tinged with awe; veneration.
- Rudiment: the elements or first principles of a subject; a mere beginning; foundation; base.

When we consider these definitions to these words and then join them together, I believe "reverent rudiments" for revival are the scripturally respected elementary principles and basic foundations rooted in the Bible that are required for us to experience revival in our lives. In

103

fact, these reverent rudiments are so important that if we do not have them in place in our lives, then we will unfortunately experience the complete opposite of revival, which would be the loss of life or destruction in our lives. This is scripturally supported when we consider Psalm 11:3 and Matthew 7:24-29 which say:

> [3] *If the foundations are destroyed,*
> *What can the righteous do?*
>
> *Psalm 11:3 NKJV*

> [24] *Therefore whoever hears these sayings of Mine, and does them, I will liken him to a wise man who built his house on the rock:* [25] *and the rain descended, the floods came, and the winds blew and beat on that house; and it did not fall, for it was founded on the rock.* [26] *"But everyone who hears these sayings of Mine, and does not do them, will be like a foolish man who built his house on the sand:* [27] *and the rain descended, the floods came, and the winds blew and beat on that house; and it fell. And great was its fall."*
> [28] *And so it was, when Jesus had ended these sayings, that the people were astonished at His teaching,* [29] *for He taught them as one having authority, and not as the scribes.*
>
> *Matthew 7:24-29 NKJV*

Consequently, we must be sure to have reverent rudiments for revival in our lives so we can avoid being destroyed and broken down. Instead, we should be well-built and raised up on the solid foundation of God's Kingdom principles, which were in place in the upper room leading up to the revival at Pentecost. After all, there is a personal cost to our Pentecost. What does that mean? It means that although our divine salvation is indeed a free gift Jesus Christ paid for at the cross for every person who calls upon His name, Christ still calls on all of us as believers to pay a personal cost for our Pentecost, also known as revival. This personal cost for Pentecost serves to position and posture us before

Him, and in Him, so we can readily receive the promised Holy Spirit He and our Heavenly Father have made available to us. In fact, this principle of paying the cost for our Pentecost can be clearly seen is several biblical passages such as Luke 9:23; 1 Corinthians 15:31, and Galatians 2:20 which say:

> *²³ Then He said to them all, "If anyone desires to come after Me, let him deny himself, and take up his cross daily, and follow Me."*
>
> *Luke 9:23 NKJV*

> *³¹ I affirm, by the boasting in you which I have in Christ Jesus our Lord, I die daily.*
>
> *1 Corinthians 15:31 NKJV*

> *²⁰ I have been crucified with Christ; it is no longer I who live, but Christ lives in me; and the life which I now live in the flesh I live by faith in the Son of God, who loved me and gave Himself for me.*
>
> *Galatians 2:20 NKJV*

Each of these New Testament biblical passages remind us that Jesus Christ Himself and the Apostle Paul calls each and every one of us to spiritually take up our cross daily, die daily to our old nature, and be crucified with Christ. In other words, in Christ, we too must pay a price.

To further prove the point of there being a personal cost to our Pentecost, we should remember that in the Old Testament books of Exodus, Numbers, and Leviticus, God revealed to the Prophet Moses the Israelites would be required to abide by sacred and certain basic, elementary, and foundational requirements. In fact, there were reverent rudiments that God specifically called them to implement in their lives in preparation for them to celebrate the festivals He instituted through Moses. These festivals included the Feast of Pentecost, also known as the Feast of Harvest or Feast of Weeks, which first began in the Old

Testament. Therefore, let us consider Exodus 23:16, Exodus 34:22, Numbers 28:26, and Leviticus 23:16 which say:

> *16 and the Feast of Harvest, the firstfruits of your labors which you have sown in the field;*
>
> *Exodus 23:16a NKJV*

> *22 "And you shall observe the Feast of Weeks, of the firstfruits of wheat harvest,*
>
> *Exodus 34:22a NKJV*

> *26 Also on the day of the firstfruits, when you bring a new grain offering to the LORD at your Feast of Weeks, you shall have a holy convocation. You shall do no customary work.*
>
> *Numbers 28:26 NKJV*

> *16 Count fifty days to the day after the seventh Sabbath; then you shall offer a new grain offering to the LORD.*
>
> *Leviticus 23:16 NKJV*

Since the first festival of Pentecost was celebrated 50 days after the first Passover, during the season of the wheat grain harvest, which normally takes place in the Gregorian calendar either at the end of May or beginning of June, God instructed Moses to tell the Israelites they were required to prepare a first-fruits offering of wheat grain to be sacrificially given by each of them to the Lord. Why? Because Pentecost required a personal cost from everyone.

Therefore, just as the Israelites of the Old Testament and the Jews of the New Testament did so, in biblical principle, we each must also do our spiritual part for our personal spiritual Pentecost. I call this "getting an alignment for the assignment," and the corresponding insight is directly related to our vehicles getting a wheel alignment for the driving assignment of transporting us from one place to another. This means that before we can receive the move of God to then move with

God, we must first move ourselves into a place before God, so we can move forward to the places and purposes God has prepared for us. The reason for this is because God requires of us to do such in preparation of receiving His Pentecost revival power.

Now, because God is extremely good to us, He additionally provides a heavenly extraordinary incentive for us to apply these spiritual personal costs for a spiritual Pentecost in our lives. This incentive not only aligns us to what God has assigned for us to experience here on earth, but it also prepares us to spiritually ascend from an upper room experience to a throne room heavenly encounter. Of course, the latter is far greater than the former. To help us biblically and spiritually understand this, we should consider Ephesians 2:4-7 and Revelation 4:1-2 which say:

> *[4] But God, who is rich in mercy, because of His great love with which He loved us, [5] even when we were dead in trespasses, made us alive together with Christ (by grace you have been saved), [6] and raised us up together, and made us sit together in the heavenly places in Christ Jesus, [7] that in the ages to come He might show the exceeding riches of His grace in His kindness toward us in Christ Jesus.*
>
> *Ephesians 2:4-7 NKJV*

> *[1] After these things I looked, and behold, a door standing open in heaven. And the first voice which I heard was like a trumpet speaking with me, saying, "Come up here, and I will show you things which must take place after this."*
> *[2] Immediately I was in the Spirit; and behold, a throne set in heaven, and One sat on the throne.*
>
> *Revelation 4:2 NKJV*

From these passages of scripture, we can discover that when we shift from upper room experiences to throne room encounters with God, then we go beyond receiving divine downloads on earth from our Lord in heaven to also participating in spiritual uploads from the earth to the heavens through our Lord Jesus Christ and His heavenly kingdom. Consequently, spiritual uploads then become accessible to a multitude of fellow believers, beyond us, who are also accessing the heavenly realms in Christ from all over our nation and throughout the earth. This heavenly incentive to pay the cost for a personal Pentecost, in principle, is especially evident in the lives of the Apostles John and Paul who not only experienced God's presence on earth, but also encountered God's glory in heaven, according to Revelation 1:9-10 and 2 Corinthians 12:1-4 which say:

> [9] *I, John, both your brother and companion in the tribulation and kingdom and patience of Jesus Christ, was on the island that is called Patmos for the word of God and for the testimony of Jesus Christ.* [10] *I was in the Spirit on the Lord's Day, and I heard behind me a loud voice, as of a trumpet,*
>
> *Revelation 1:9-10 NKJV*

> [1] *It is doubtless not profitable for me to boast. I will come to visions and Revelation of the Lord:* [2] *I know a man in Christ who fourteen years ago—whether in the body I do not know, or whether out of the body I do not know, God knows—such a one was caught up to the third heaven.* [3] *And I know such a man—whether in the body or out of the body I do not know, God knows—* [4] *how he was caught up into Paradise and heard inexpressible words, which it is not lawful for a man to utter.*
>
> *2 Corinthians 12:1-4 NKJV*

Additionally, it is profoundly important to note that only in Jesus Christ, and only by His invitation to us, can we spiritually rise above time and space to sit with Him and our Heavenly Father, where they are seated on their thrones of grace and glory, ruling and reigning in an everlasting now, according to Revelation 3:21 and Colossians 3:1-4 which say:

> *²¹ To him who overcomes I will grant to sit with Me on My throne, as I also overcame and sat down with My Father on His throne.*
>
> *Revelation 3:21 NKJV*

> *¹ If then you were raised with Christ, seek those things which are above, where Christ is, sitting at the right hand of God. ² Set your mind on things above, not on things on the earth. ³ For you died, and your life is hidden with Christ in God. ⁴ When Christ who is our life appears, then you also will appear with Him in glory.*
>
> *Colossians 3:1-4 NKJV*

Subsequently, it is there, in God's heavenly throne room, and in Christ Jesus, where we are able to spiritually access all He has already made available for us in the heavenlies, so we can then have it manifested and demonstrated here on earth. In fact, I believe Jesus Christ made that throne room accessibility available to the Apostle Peter, before Christ ever made it available to the Apostles John and Paul. I believe this, because Jesus Christ first gave the keys of the kingdom of heaven to Peter, according to Matthew 16:18-19 which says:

> *¹⁸ And I also say to you that you are Peter, and on this rock I will build My church, and the gates of Hades shall not prevail against it. ¹⁹ And I will give you the keys of the kingdom of heaven, and whatever you bind on earth will be bound in heaven, and whatever you loose on earth will be loosed in heaven.*
>
> *Matthew 16:18-19 NKJV*

With that in mind, since our Heavenly Father is no respecter of persons, I also believe that, only in Christ Jesus, He has also made it available for you and me in our post-modern times. All we have to do is pay the cost for our personal Pentecost by applying the reverent rudiments for revival to our lives. When we do, then we can prepare to spiritually rise to higher heights in Jesus Christ and see His Spirit poured out upon and through our lives like never before. So what are the reverent rudiments for revival according to Acts 1:1-8, 1:12-20, and 2:1 which we read at the beginning of this chapter? The five rudiments for revival are:

1. PRAYER
2. FASTING
3. WORSHIP
4. LIVING ACCORDING TO GOD'S WORD
5. UNITY

Now, because each of these reverent rudiments for revival rightfully deserve our focused attention on each of them, instead of covering them all in the next chapter, I will intentionally take the next five chapters to focus on each of them individually. Together, they will collectively reveal how we can personally pay the cost for our personal Pentecost which can result in a corporate Pentecost for all. Therefore, please join me in the next chapter to find out all about the first reverent rudiment for revival, which is prayer. History is in the making for the next great awakening, and it is time for us to apply to our lives the reverent rudiments of revival that will position and posture us to receive revival now!

CHAPTER 7
THE RUDIMENT OF PRAYER

When I consider the word of God as it relevantly and reverently relates to the revival the primitive church experienced on the Day of Pentecost, together with my personal experience of revival, I believe the first of five rudiments for revival is prayer. This rudiment is biblically based on Acts 1:12-14, in addition to many other passages of scriptures I will share in this chapter. Consider the following:

> *¹² Then they returned to Jerusalem from the mount called Olivet, which is near Jerusalem, a Sabbath day's journey. ¹³ And when they had entered, they went up into the upper room where they were staying: Peter, James, John, and Andrew; Philip and Thomas; Bartholomew and Matthew; James the son of Alphaeus and Simon the Zealot; and Judas the son of James. ¹⁴ These all continued with one accord in prayer and supplication, with the women and Mary the mother of Jesus, and with His brothers.*
>
> *Acts 1:12-14 NKJV*

111

In this passage of scripture, we see that one of the very first things Peter and the 120 disciples did in preparing and posturing themselves to receive revival on the Day of Pentecost was to pray. Additional biblical passages prove just how extremely important prayer is, in order for there to be revival in our lives. One of them is registered in Matthew 6:5-13, where our Lord Jesus Christ himself says the following to the twelve disciples with whom he started His earthly ministry:

> [5] *And when you pray, you shall not be like the hypocrites. For they love to pray standing in the synagogues and on the corners of the streets, that they may be seen by men. Assuredly, I say to you, they have their reward.* [6] *But you, when you pray, go into your room, and when you have shut your door, pray to your Father who is in the secret place; and your Father who sees in secret will reward you openly.* [7] *And when you pray, do not use vain repetitions as the heathen do. For they think that they will be heard for their many words.*
> [8] *"Therefore do not be like them. For your Father knows the things you have need of before you ask Him.* [9] *In this manner, therefore, pray:*
> *Our Father in heaven,*
> *Hallowed be Your name.*
> [10] *Your kingdom come.*
> *Your will be done*
> *On earth as it is in heaven.*
> [11] *Give us this day our daily bread.*
> [12] *And forgive us our debts,*
> *As we forgive our debtors.*
> [13] *And do not lead us into temptation,*
> *But deliver us from the evil one.*
> *For Yours is the kingdom and the power and the glory forever. Amen.*

Matthew 6:5-13 NKJV

Here, Jesus Christ, near the beginning of His earthly ministry, teaches His twelve disciples, and now us as His followers, that prayer, is not a matter of "if," but rather a mandate of "when." In fact, Jesus Christ teaches us prayer should not be limited to a few minutes, done three times a day before our meals or at the beginning and end of our day. Later, nearing the end of His earthly ministry, Christ reiterates the importance of prayer, especially in the lives of His disciples, and now in ours, when He says the following in Matthew 26:36-46 which is re-emphasized in Mark 14:32-42:

> [36] *Then Jesus went with his disciples to a place called Gethsemane, and he said to them, "Sit here while I go over there and pray."* [37] *He took Peter and the two sons of Zebedee along with him, and he began to be sorrowful and troubled.* [38] *Then he said to them, "My soul is overwhelmed with sorrow to the point of death. Stay here and keep watch with me."*
> [39] *Going a little farther, he fell with his face to the ground and prayed, "My Father, if it is possible, may this cup be taken from me. Yet not as I will, but as you will."*
> [40] *Then he returned to his disciples and found them sleeping. "Couldn't you men keep watch with me for one hour?" he asked Peter.* [41] *"Watch and pray so that you will not fall into temptation. The spirit is willing, but the flesh is weak."*
> [42] *He went away a second time and prayed, "My Father, if it is not possible for this cup to be taken away unless I drink it, may your will be done."*
> [43] *When he came back, he again found them sleeping, because their eyes were heavy.* [44] *So he left them and went away once more and prayed the third time, saying the same thing.*

[45] Then he returned to the disciples and said to them, "Are you still sleeping and resting? Look, the hour has come, and the Son of Man is delivered into the hands of sinners. [46] Rise! Let us go! Here comes my betrayer!"

Matthew 26:36-46 NIV

[32] They went to a place called Gethsemane, and Jesus said to his disciples, "Sit here while I pray." [33] He took Peter, James and John along with him, and he began to be deeply distressed and troubled. [34] "My soul is overwhelmed with sorrow to the point of death," he said to them. "Stay here and keep watch."

[35] Going a little farther, he fell to the ground and prayed that if possible the hour might pass from him. [36] "Abba, Father," he said, "everything is possible for you. Take this cup from me. Yet not what I will, but what you will."

[37] Then he returned to his disciples and found them sleeping. "Simon," he said to Peter, "are you asleep? Couldn't you keep watch for one hour? [38] Watch and pray so that you will not fall into temptation. The spirit is willing, but the flesh is weak."

[39] Once more he went away and prayed the same thing. [40] When he came back, he again found them sleeping, because their eyes were heavy. They did not know what to say to him.

[41] Returning the third time, he said to them, "Are you still sleeping and resting? Enough! The hour has come. Look, the Son of Man is delivered into the hands of sinners. [42] Rise! Let us go! Here comes my betrayer!"

Mark 14:32-42 NIV

In these scriptural passages, our Lord Jesus Christ teaches us prayer is a rudiment that has the potential of keeping us from physically and spiritually falling asleep and consequently falling into carnal

114

temptations. Why is this the case? Prayer has the potential to awaken our spirit to what God is saying and doing in the most difficult and desperate of times, such as the current COVID-19 growing global pandemic and the increasingly rising racial tensions occurring throughout our nation. Additionally, prayer can administer revival power into the lives of others. This was evident in and through the life of the Apostle Peter in Acts 9:36-42 when God used Peter's prayer life to revive the life of Tabitha, also known as Dorcas, in a different upper room from the one Peter and the 120 disciples had gone to in Acts 1. Consider Acts 9:36-42 which says:

> [36] *At Joppa there was a certain disciple named Tabitha, which is translated Dorcas. This woman was full of good works and charitable deeds which she did.* [37] *But it happened in those days that she became sick and died. When they had washed her, they laid her in an upper room.* [38] *And since Lydda was near Joppa, and the disciples had heard that Peter was there, they sent two men to him, imploring him not to delay in coming to them.* [39] *Then Peter arose and went with them. When he had come, they brought him to the upper room. And all the widows stood by him weeping, showing the tunics and garments which Dorcas had made while she was with them.* [40] *But Peter put them all out, and knelt down and prayed. And turning to the body he said, "Tabitha, arise." And she opened her eyes, and when she saw Peter she sat up.* [41] *Then he gave her his hand and lifted her up; and when he had called the saints and widows, he presented her alive.* [42] *And it became known throughout all Joppa, and many believed on the Lord.*
>
> *Acts 9:36-42 NKJV*

This is such a powerful example of the revival power of prayer. Additionally, when we consider the life and ministry of the Old Testament Prophets Elijah and Elisha, we can see prayer is what God used to usher in revival into the lives of others around them, based on what supernaturally happened in the lives of dead people as registered in 1 Kings 17:17-24 and 2 Kings 4:27-37 which say:

> *[17] Now it happened after these things that the son of the woman who owned the house became sick. And his sickness was so serious that there was no breath left in him. [18] So she said to Elijah, "What have I to do with you, O man of God? Have you come to me to bring my sin to remembrance, and to kill my son?"*
>
> *[19] And he said to her, "Give me your son." So he took him out of her arms and carried him to the upper room where he was staying, and laid him on his own bed. [20] Then he cried out to the LORD and said, "O LORD my God, have You also brought tragedy on the widow with whom I lodge, by killing her son?" [21] And he stretched himself out on the child three times, and cried out to the LORD and said, "O LORD my God, I pray, let this child's soul come back to him." [22] Then the LORD heard the voice of Elijah; and the soul of the child came back to him, and he revived.*
>
> *[23] And Elijah took the child and brought him down from the upper room into the house, and gave him to his mother. And Elijah said, "See, your son lives!"*
>
> *[24] Then the woman said to Elijah, "Now by this I know that you are a man of God, and that the word of the LORD in your mouth is the truth."*
>
> *1 Kings 17:17-24 NKJV*

> *[27] When she reached the man of God at the mountain, she took hold of his feet. Gehazi came over to push her away, but the man of God said, "Leave her alone! She is in bitter distress, but the LORD has hidden it from me and has not told me why."*

116

²⁸ *"Did I ask you for a son, my lord?" she said. "Didn't I tell you, 'Don't raise my hopes'?"*
²⁹ *Elisha said to Gehazi, "Tuck your cloak into your belt, take my staff in your hand and run. Don't greet anyone you meet, and if anyone greets you, do not answer. Lay my staff on the boy's face."*
³⁰ *But the child's mother said, "As surely as the LORD lives and as you live, I will not leave you." So he got up and followed her.*
³¹ *Gehazi went on ahead and laid the staff on the boy's face, but there was no sound or response. So Gehazi went back to meet Elisha and told him, "The boy has not awakened."*
³² *When Elisha reached the house, there was the boy lying dead on his couch.* ³³ *He went in, shut the door on the two of them and prayed to the LORD.* ³⁴ *Then he got on the bed and lay on the boy, mouth to mouth, eyes to eyes, hands to hands. As he stretched himself out on him, the boy's body grew warm.* ³⁵ *Elisha turned away and walked back and forth in the room and then got on the bed and stretched out on him once more. The boy sneezed seven times and opened his eyes.*
³⁶ *Elisha summoned Gehazi and said, "Call the Shunammite." And he did. When she came, he said, "Take your son."* ³⁷ *She came in, fell at his feet and bowed to the ground. Then she took her son and went out.*

2 Kings 4:27-37 NIV

This is absolutely amazing. Can you imagine what that revival experience must have been like for these prophets who prayed and for the children who were revived because of the revival prayers that were prayed? From these passages of scripture especially from 1 Kings 17, it is clear that revival can come through the reverent rudiment of prayer. In fact, I believe Elijah's prayer life, which God used to revive the widow's son, provides us with four spiritual steps towards a supernatural upper room experience for others, when we pray for them to be revived spiritually and supernaturally. These prayer steps are the following:

1. We must begin by crying out to God in prayer for revival for all generations, especially for the younger generations.
2. We must take the younger generations to our spiritual upper rooms of prayer and continuously cover them completely in prayer from head to toe.
3. We must specifically pray for their revival, with an expectation that God will hear us and respond to us.
4. We must believe God will gracefully use us to return a revived and living generation to its parents.

After all, throughout bible and post-bible history, it has been undeniably notable that prayer is what predicates, sustains, and maintains revival. With all due respect to us preachers, I have learned over my 23 years of ministry that God's preachers do not necessarily bring revival, as much as the prayers of God's preachers and His people do. In fact, although in my prior pastorates, I loved having guest speakers minister in special services, and although I enjoy being a guest speaker myself for Pastors in their special events, I have learned a sobering truth. Greater than the 30-60-minute preaching of us invited guest speakers, is the intercessory groaning spirit of the people who pray for revival over the course of hours, days, weeks, months, and even years. In fact, this has been confirmed by great revivalists such as Duncan Campbell of the 1949 Hebrides Revival who said:

> *It is one thing to shout about it, it is one thing to sing it, it is one thing to talk about revival, but give me a people on their faces, seeking to be rightly related with God, and when that happens, we will soon know the impact of God-realization in our country.*[1]
>
> *Duncan Campbell, 1949 Hebrides Revival*

Interestingly enough, the Hebrides revival was started by two elderly ladies in their 80s who decided in their era that it was time for revival now. Subsequently, it was their prayers that predicated, sustained, and caused revival to remain. Therefore, I believe God is now searching for godly people of all ages, ethnicities, and nationalities in His kingdom who will pray just as they did in many of the revivals of the past 300 years. In fact, one of the greatest revivals that contributed to other revivals throughout the world was the 1904 Welsh Revival, which I briefly mentioned in the third chapter of this book.

Since this revival was so impactful, it bears repeating that it was led by a 26-year old young man by the name of Evan Roberts. He, for many months before the revival began, would spend hours on end each day praying for his own personal revival. Thereafter, when he went to Bible college, he began to pray with a small group of other young adults. Soon after, he returned to his home church to have revival youth services which were predicated by separate prayer services, and then followed by post-prayer services. These prayer services before and after the regular services were at least one to two hours long, and sometimes even longer. It was the supernatural influence of these prolonged prayer services that ushered in revival into the lives of youth and young adults which eventually spread to the adults in their congregation and thereafter to other congregations in their city, region, country, and the rest of the world. Their prayers were paramount in conceiving, carrying, and birthing a local revival which resulted in a global revival.

Now what would happen if the modern-day youth and young adult generation were to begin to pray more than they play? In order to receive revival now we must go beyond having a playing generation to having a praying generation. In fact, with all of the shelter-in-place orders understandably having been made throughout our nation and the rest of the world, I believe now is not the time for our young people to spend hours on end, until the break of day, playing video games in their rooms. Instead, I believe this could be one of the greatest times for them to invest hours throughout each day praying in their rooms until they experience a spiritual upper room. Additionally, whenever our nation and the rest of the world returns to a new normal in the near future, the reality is that all generations, especially the younger generation, will understandably return to spending a lot of time playing extra-curricular activities both on and off of the field. However, as much as I personally enjoy playing and watching sports and other sorts of gaming, I also realize that we, the Church, must get back to praying now more than ever. If all generations are not careful, we will allow all of our joyful playing to get in the way of our needful praying.

Therefore, there can be no excuses for not praying. On the contrary, there must be an increased expectation for praying, especially when we consider God's word in James 5:17-18 which says:

> *[17] Elijah was a man with a nature like ours, and he prayed earnestly that it would not rain; and it did not rain on the land for three years and six months. [18] And he prayed again, and the heaven gave rain, and the earth produced its fruit.*
> *James 5:17-18 NKJV*

Here we see that Elijah was human, just like us, and he dealt with temptations like we deal with today. But because he prayed, God listened, and because God listened, God responded with rains that revived the earth to produce much needed fruit in his time. Hence, I believe it is time we begin to pray like Elijah prayed. Yet this time, the much-needed fruit we need to be produced in the earth is for something far greater than physical food. What we need in the earth is a spiritual revival for our nation and the rest of the world. In fact, because of the new covenant brought to us through the precious blood of Jesus Christ, our prayers can bring forth greater results because of the better covenant that is found in Jesus' precious blood.

When I consider this, it reminds me of how the prayer life of two of Cornerstone Church's youth leaders, Priscilla Serrano and Lissette Gonzalez "then Navarrete" resulted in them specifically praying for Madison High School in San Antonio, Texas. They prayed for the continuation of a Bible study club our youth ministry had established there through one of our prior leaders Christian Londoño. Due to their collective prayers, we were able to continue the bible study club at Madison High School. Soon thereafter, in the Fall Semester of 2010, during one of their club meetings and prayer times in the school's Orchestra Room, they prayed for a creative miracle to occur in the life of a high school student named Jessica Sousa. Making a long story short, they prayed, in faith believing, that God could cause Jessica's right leg to grow out two inches longer to match the length of her left leg. As they prayed with several other young people in the room, God responded and Jessica's right leg grew out to the same length as her left leg. It was a supernatural surreal miraculous moment, to say the least.

Interestingly enough, before that miracle happened, over the course of approximately six months prior, for one hour before our youth services, our youth staff and youth leaders had been praying for all of our students and their schools throughout San Antonio. Thus, it was obvious to us that all of the cumulative prayers of our staff, leaders, and even some of our youth was making an impact in their generation and in their schools. After that miracle happened, we continued praying for more of what God had in store for those who would pray, not play. The results were glorious as students at Madison High School and other schools throughout San Antonio were being healed, saved, and touched by the power of God through prayers that were ushering in revival into the younger generation.

Now returning to the rudiment of prayer, I also believe that if we will begin to pray, then we will begin to see God's glory over this generation like never before, according to Luke 9:28-32 which says:

> *[28] Now it came to pass, about eight days after these sayings, that He took Peter, John, and James and went up on the mountain to pray. [29] As He prayed, the appearance of His face was altered, and His robe became white and glistening. [30] And behold, two men talked with Him, who were Moses and Elijah, [31] who appeared in glory and spoke of His decease which He was about to accomplish at Jerusalem.*

121

^{32} But Peter and those with him were heavy with sleep; and when they were fully awake, they saw His glory and the two men who stood with Him.

Luke 9:28-32 NKJV

When I consider this passage of scripture, I believe God wants us to behold what He has already made available to us. Hence, we must spiritually awaken in prayer to see it with our own eyes. Subsequently, we cannot forget that revival is completely conditional, as clearly explained in 2 Chronicles 7:14 which says:

^{14} if My people who are called by My name will humble themselves, and pray and seek My face, and turn from their wicked ways, then I will hear from heaven, and will forgive their sin and heal their land.

2 Chronicles 7:14 NKJV

Consequently, we must do our part in prayer, if we expect God to do His part in power.

Now with regards to us doing our part in prayer, our prayers must begin with repentance as noted in 2 Chronicles 7:14 and many other scriptures in the Bible such as Acts 2, 3, 11, 17, 2 Peter 3, and Revelation 3. Let us consider these scripture passages in light of the importance of making sure repentance is the initial part of our prayers for revival.

^{38} Then Peter said to them, "Repent, and let every one of you be baptized in the name of Jesus Christ for the remission of sins; and you shall receive the gift of the Holy Spirit."

Acts 2:38 NKJV

^{19} Repent therefore and be converted, that your sins may be blotted out, so that times of refreshing may come from the presence of the Lord, ^{20} and that He may send Jesus Christ,

122

who was preached to you before, ^{21} whom heaven must receive until the times of restoration of all things, which God has spoken by the mouth of all His holy prophets since the world began.

Acts 3:19-21 NKJV

^{9} The Lord is not slack concerning His promise, as some count slackness, but is longsuffering toward us, not willing that any should perish but that all should come to repentance.

2 Peter 3:9 NKJV

^{17} "If therefore God gave them the same gift as He gave us when we believed on the Lord Jesus Christ, who was I that I could withstand God?" ^{18} When they heard these things they became silent; and they glorified God, saying, "Then God has also granted to the Gentiles repentance to life."

Acts 11:17-18 NKJV

^{30} Truly, these times of ignorance God overlooked, but now commands all men everywhere to repent, ^{31} because He has appointed a day on which He will judge the world in righteousness by the Man whom He has ordained. He has given assurance of this to all by raising Him from the dead.

Acts 17:30-31 NKJV

^{19} As many as I love, I rebuke and chasten. Therefore be zealous and repent.

Revelation 3:19 NKJV

Based on these passages of scriptures, and so many more throughout the entire Bible, I wholeheartedly believe that now more than ever before, we need to pray, and in our prayers, we must repent. Correspondingly, we should remember that repentance is not a curse, but

123

rather a blessing. In fact, repentance is a great privilege God grants us to do for our own benefit according to His will for us. Repentance causes people to return to the Lord and position themselves to receive the release of times of refreshing from the Lord. The undeniable biblical reality is that if we will repent, then God will release revival to us. In fact, our repentance in prayer will position and posture us to receive God's kingdom as noted in Matthew 4:17 and Mark 1:14-15 which say:

> *[17] From that time Jesus began to preach and to say,*
> *"Repent, for the kingdom of heaven is at hand."*
>
> *Matthew 4:17 NKJV*

> *[14] Now after John was put in prison, Jesus came to Galilee,*
> *preaching the gospel of the kingdom of God, [15] and saying,*
> *"The time is fulfilled, and the kingdom of God is at hand.*
> *Repent, and believe in the gospel."*
>
> *Mark 1:14-15 NKJV*

When we receive God's kingdom through our repentance in prayer, then we will be able to effectively pray for others through intercession so they can receive the same kingdom of God with revival power. However, repentance must start with us as Jesus Christ taught in Luke 13:1-5 which says:

> *[13] There were present at that season some who told Him*
> *about the Galileans whose blood Pilate had mingled with*
> *their sacrifices. [2] And Jesus answered and said to them,*
> *"Do you suppose that these Galileans were worse sinners*
> *than all other Galileans, because they suffered such things?*
> *[3] I tell you, no; but unless you repent you will all likewise*
> *perish. [4] Or those eighteen on whom the tower in Siloam fell*
> *and killed them, do you think that they were worse sinners*
> *than all other men who dwelt in Jerusalem? [5] I tell you, no;*
> *but unless you repent you will all likewise perish."*

Luke 13:1-5 NKJV

In this passage, our Lord Jesus Christ makes it crystal clear that repentance is vital in our prayer for revival. Therefore, the question bears asking: "What does it truly mean to repent?" The Greek word for repent is "metanoeo," which literally means to change the way we think so we can change the way we live. It is connected to what the Apostle Paul wrote in Romans 12:2 which says:

2 And do not be conformed to this world, but be transformed by the renewing of your mind, that you may prove what is that good and acceptable and perfect will of God.
Romans 12:2 NKJV

Additionally, the word "repent" can be understood by what its two parts reveal, "re" and "pent, " "re" meaning again and "pent" meaning top. Therefore, considering both the Greek and English words for "repent," to repent could mean to change the way a person thinks in order to get back on top again. This can be fully understood when we consider that humanity fell in the garden of Eden in Genesis 3. There Adam and Eve allowed their thinking and living to be changed by the enemy serpent who deceived them into thinking and living differently from what God originally intended for them to think and live like. However, when we begin to repent through our prayers based on God's word, then a glorious revival begins to take place in our lives, and we begin to get back on top again through thinking and living in the manner in which God and Jesus Christ calls us to.

Additionally, when we begin to repent in prayer, then we can proceed to also repent in intercession for others through our prayers just like Abraham did for Lot, his family, and the two cities of Sodom and Gomorrah, according to Genesis 18:16-33 which says:

16 When the men got up to leave, they looked down toward Sodom, and Abraham walked along with them to see them on their way. ¹⁷ Then the LORD said, "Shall I hide from Abraham what I am about to do? ¹⁸ Abraham will surely become a great and powerful nation, and all nations on earth will be blessed through him. ¹⁹ For I have chosen him, so that he will direct his children and his household after him to keep the way of the LORD by doing what is right and just, so that the LORD will bring about for Abraham what he has promised him."

²⁰ Then the LORD said, "The outcry against Sodom and Gomorrah is so great and their sin so grievous ²¹ that I will go down and see if what they have done is as bad as the outcry that has reached me. If not, I will know."

²² The men turned away and went toward Sodom, but Abraham remained standing before the LORD. ²³ Then Abraham approached him and said: "Will you sweep away the righteous with the wicked? ²⁴ What if there are fifty righteous people in the city? Will you really sweep it away and not spare the place for the sake of the fifty righteous people in it? ²⁵ Far be it from you to do such a thing—to kill the righteous with the wicked, treating the righteous and the wicked alike. Far be it from you! Will not the Judge of all the earth do right?"

²⁶ The LORD said, "If I find fifty righteous people in the city of Sodom, I will spare the whole place for their sake."

²⁷ Then Abraham spoke up again: "Now that I have been so bold as to speak to the Lord, though I am nothing but dust and ashes, ²⁸ what if the number of the righteous is five less than fifty? Will you destroy the whole city for lack of five people?"

"If I find forty-five there," he said, "I will not destroy it."

²⁹ Once again he spoke to him, "What if only forty are found there?"

He said, "For the sake of forty, I will not do it."

³⁰ Then he said, "May the Lord not be angry, but let me
speak. What if only thirty can be found there?"
He answered, "I will not do it if I find thirty there."
³¹ Abraham said, "Now that I have been so bold as to speak
to the Lord, what if only twenty can be found there?"
He said, "For the sake of twenty, I will not destroy it."
³² Then he said, "May the Lord not be angry, but let me
speak just once more. What if only ten can be found there?"
He answered, "For the sake of ten, I will not destroy it."
³³ When the LORD had finished speaking with Abraham, he
left, and Abraham returned home.

Genesis 18:16-33 NIV

From this passage of scripture, we can conclude that if God was willing to spare all of Sodom and Gomorrah in Genesis 18 due to the lives of ten righteous people who unfortunately could not be found in those two cities, then imagine the glorious kind of kingdom revival God could bring to our cities, regions, states, our nation and beyond, due to all of our prayers of intercession and repentance.

Consequently, as we pray, we should remember that according to Romans 8, we are not praying alone or just with each other. As powerful as that is, the even more powerful reality is that both Jesus Christ and the Holy Spirit have already been praying and interceding for the Church, our generations, our nation, and the nations of the world. Now God is waiting on us to join His Son and His Spirit in prayer and intercession for others according to Romans 8:26, 34 which says:

²⁶ Likewise the Spirit also helps in our weaknesses. For we
do not know what we should pray for as we ought, but the
Spirit Himself makes intercession for us with groanings
which cannot be uttered.

[34] Who is he who condemns? It is Christ who died, and furthermore is also risen, who is even at the right hand of God, who also makes intercession for us.

Romans 8:26, 34 NKJV

Correspondingly and respectfully, I must point out that the language in which Jesus Christ and the Holy Spirit are praying and interceding in is a heavenly or spiritual language, that we, in our humanity, are not able to know nor pray humanly. However, the great news is that we are invited by God's word to also pray and intercede in His heavenly or spiritual language according to Ephesians 6:16 and 1 Corinthians 14:14 which say:

[18] praying always with all prayer and supplication in the Spirit, being watchful to this end with all perseverance and supplication for all the saints—

Ephesians 6:16 NKJV

[14] For if I pray in a tongue, my spirit prays, but my understanding is unfruitful. [15] What is the conclusion then? I will pray with the spirit, and I will also pray with the understanding. I will sing with the spirit, and I will also sing with the understanding.

1 Corinthians 14:14 NKJV

Therefore, I believe that now is the time for us to join Jesus Christ and the Holy Spirit in prayer and intercession like never before in both our earthly languages and in His heavenly language. When we do so, I believe we will position and posture ourselves to receive revival for our generations, nation, and beyond. One of the major reasons for this is due to the divine confidence God has given to us through the writings of the Apostle John in 1 John 5:14-15 which says:

128

[14] Now this is the confidence that we have in Him, that if we ask anything according to His will, He hears us. [15] And if we know that He hears us, whatever we ask, we know that we have the petitions that we have asked of Him.

1 John 5:14-15 NKJV

Finally, as we pray, I believe it would be beneficial for us to acknowledge and apply what our Lord Jesus Christ showed me in 2002 to be the 10 Pillars of Prayer according to Matthew 6:9-13 which says:

[9] In this manner, therefore, pray:
Our Father in heaven,
Hallowed be Your name.
[10] Your kingdom come.
Your will be done
On earth as it is in heaven.
[11] Give us this day our daily bread.
[12] And forgive us our debts,
As we forgive our debtors.
[13] And do not lead us into temptation,
But deliver us from the evil one.
For Yours is the kingdom and the power and the glory
forever. Amen.

Matthew 6:9-13 NKJV

In this passage of scripture, the Lord's Prayer reveals to us what I call the 10 Pillars of Prayer which are:

1. God's Person, which reveals who He is to us: "[9] Our Father..."
2. God's Place, which reveals where He reigns from: "in heaven..."
3. God's Praise, which reveals what He is worthy of: "Hallowed be Your name..."
4. God's Purpose, which reveals what He focuses on: "[10] Your kingdom come. Your will be done..."

5. God's Plan, which reveals how He works: "On earth as *it is* in heaven..."

6. God's Provision, which reveals what He can give us: "[11] Give us this day our daily bread..."

7. God's Pardon, which reveals how merciful He is to us: "[12] And forgive us our debts, As we forgive our debtors..."

8. God's Protection, which reveals how He guards us: "[13] And do not lead us into temptation..."

9. God's Power, which reveals how He enables us: "But deliver us from the evil one..."

10. God's Possessions, which reveals what He has for us: "For Yours is the kingdom and the power and the glory forever. Amen."

Now when we pray with this biblical understanding, together with praying in His Spirit, then I believe we can expect to receive what the Apostle Peter, the other apostles, and the rapidly increasing number of disciples received in their time of prayer, according to Acts 4:23-31 which says:

> [23] *And being let go, they went to their own companions and reported all that* the chief *priests and elders had said to them.* [24] *So when they heard that, they raised their voice to God with one accord and said: "Lord, You are God, who made heaven and earth and the sea, and all that is in them,* [25] *who by the mouth of Your servant David have said:*
> *'Why did the nations rage,*
> *And the people plot vain things?*
> [26] *The kings of the earth took their stand,*
> *And the rulers were gathered together*
> *Against the LORD and against His Christ.'*
> [27] *"For truly against Your holy Servant Jesus, whom You anointed, both Herod and Pontius Pilate, with the Gentiles and the people of Israel, were gathered together* [28] *to do*

whatever Your hand and Your purpose determined before to be done. [29] Now, Lord, look on their threats, and grant to Your servants that with all boldness they may speak Your word, [30] by stretching out Your hand to heal, and that signs and wonders may be done through the name of Your holy Servant Jesus."

[31] And when they had prayed, the place where they were assembled together was shaken; and they were all filled with the Holy Spirit, and they spoke the word of God with boldness.

Acts 4:23-31 NKJV

What a glorious experience that must have been for Peter and the believers in Acts 4, and what a glorious experience it will be for you and me in 2020 and onward. Get ready, because I believe our Bible-based, faith-filled, Christ-centered, Spirit-filled, and Spirit-led prayers are about to provoke our God to move heaven and earth for His glory. May we pray, "O Lord, shake us 'till you wake us," and may He use our prayers for repentance, intercession, and the ushering in of His heavenly blessings upon the earth once again. History is in the making for the next great awakening, and your and my prayers are about to usher in revival now!

CHAPTER 8
THE RUDIMENT OF FASTING

I have learned from God's word and my personal experience that the second of five revival rudiments is fasting. Although the word "fasting" does not appear in Acts 1 or 2, as it pertains to the account of the Apostle Peter and the 120 disciples, a close examination of what was taking place in the lives of Peter and the 120 disciples for 9 days leading up to the Day of Pentecost will reveal how, more than likely, they were indeed conducting a fast of some sort during this time period. At the very least, they were abstaining from certain human privileges in preparation to receive the promised Holy Spirit that Jesus Christ told them to go wait for in Jerusalem.

To help us understand this, it is important to clarify that fasting literally means to cover our mouths in order to keep us from eating and/or drinking something, so we can focus on spiritually eating and drinking from God's word and His Spirit. Also, it is of utmost importance for us to comprehend that fasting is a spiritual rudiment our Lord Jesus Christ taught His disciples about, as noted in Matthew 6:16-18 which says:

[16] Moreover, when you fast, do not be like the hypocrites, with a sad countenance. For they disfigure their faces that they may appear to men to be fasting. Assuredly, I say to you, they have their reward. [17] But you, when you fast, anoint your head and wash your face, [18] so that you do not appear to men to be fasting, but to your Father who is in the secret place; and your Father who sees in secret will reward you openly.

Matthew 6:16-18 NKJV

In this passage of scripture, Jesus Christ taught His disciples that fasting, like prayer, is not a matter of "if" but "when." Additionally, it is paramount to remember that Jesus Christ later taught His disciples fasting would be an expectation He would eventually have of them, especially after His ascension to the right hand of His Heavenly Father, as revealed in Matthew 9:14-15 which says:

[14] Then the disciples of John came to Him, saying, "Why do we and the Pharisees fast often, but Your disciples do not fast?"
[15] And Jesus said to them, "Can the friends of the bridegroom mourn as long as the bridegroom is with them? But the days will come when the bridegroom will be taken away from them, and then they will fast."

Matthew 9:14-15 NKJV

Furthermore, it is important to observe in Luke 22 that Jesus Christ had eaten His last Passover meal in the same upper room Peter and the 120 disciples went to in Acts 1. Interestingly enough, this particular meal of Jesus with His twelve disciples, widely known as the "Lord's Supper," occurred approximately 51 days before the Day of Pentecost. It was during this meal that Christ told His twelve disciples that He would not eat it again, until it would be fulfilled in the kingdom of God. Why is this important? Because Christ's statement revealed that

134

He would fast this particular meal for the following 2,000 years plus. This can be clearly noted in Luke 22:14-19 which says:

> *14 When the hour had come, He sat down, and the twelve apostles with Him. 15 Then He said to them, "With fervent desire I have desired to eat this Passover with you before I suffer; 16 for I say to you, I will no longer eat of it until it is fulfilled in the kingdom of God."*
> *17 Then He took the cup, and gave thanks, and said, "Take this and divide it among yourselves; 18 for I say to you, I will not drink of the fruit of the vine until the kingdom of God comes."*
> *19 And He took bread, gave thanks and broke it, and gave it to them, saying, "This is My body which is given for you; do this in remembrance of Me."*
>
> *Luke 22:14-19 NKJV*

Now when I consider all of those very important observations, I believe it reveals to us that the Apostle Peter and the 120 disciples were, in a sense or perhaps even in fact, fasting during their 9 days in the upper room leading up to the Day of Pentecost. Therefore, it strongly appears to me that fasting is a reverent rudiment for revival. In fact, I believe it is a rudiment that God had 1) originally established for His people in the Old Testament, 2) reiterated to His people throughout the New Testament, and 3) has continued to call His people to throughout the world until the rapture of the Church occurs. Why until the rapture occurs? When it does happen, Jesus Christ will break His current fast and eat the Passover meal again with His disciples at the wedding supper of the Lamb, as mentioned in Revelation 19:6-9 which says:

> *6 And I heard, as it were, the voice of a great multitude, as the sound of many waters and as the sound of mighty thunderings, saying, "Alleluia! For the Lord God Omnipotent reigns! 7 Let us be glad and rejoice and give*

Him glory, for the marriage of the Lamb has come, and His
wife has made herself ready." [8] And to her it was granted to
be arrayed in fine linen, clean and bright, for the fine linen
is the righteous acts of the saints.
[9] Then he said to me, "Write: 'Blessed are those who are
called to the marriage supper of the Lamb!' " And he said
to me, "These are the true sayings of God."

Revelation 19:6-9 NKJV

With all that said, the questions that now bear asking are: "What is fasting?" "How does it work?" "What are the results of fasting?" The answer to these three very important questions are found in what God has revealed to me to be "3-Dimensional Fasting." This 3D Fasting has to do with the three distinct connotations of the word and prefix of "fast." Additionally, it has to do with each of their different significances and the three-dimensional insight they collectively provide to what fasting is, what it does, and what we can expect to receive from it. Consider the following:

- 1st dimension of a fast: "fast" can mean to "abstain" from physical food for the sole purpose of eating spiritual food from God's word, as noted in Job 23:12 which says:

[12] I have not departed from the commandment of His lips;
I have treasured the words of His mouth
More than my necessary food.

Job 23:12 NKJV

- 2nd dimension of a fast: "fast(en)" can mean to "attach" ourselves to God for the sole purpose of knowing Him more intimately and affectionately, as noted in Isaiah 55:6 and James 4:8 which say:

⁶ Seek the LORD while He may be found,
Call upon Him while He is near.

Isaiah 55:6 NKJV

⁸ Draw near to God and He will draw near to you. Cleanse
your hands, you sinners; and purify your hearts, you
double-minded.

James 4:8 NKJV

• 3rd dimension of a fast: "fast(er)" can mean to "accelerate" the
work of God for the sole purpose of having His kingdom come
and His will be done here on earth as it is in heaven, as noted in
Isaiah 58:6-8 which says:

⁶ Is this not the fast that I have chosen:
To loose the bonds of wickedness,
To undo the heavy burdens,
To let the oppressed go free,
And that you break every yoke?
⁷ Is it not to share your bread with the hungry,
And that you bring to your house the poor who are cast out;
When you see the naked, that you cover him,
And not hide yourself from your own flesh?
⁸ Then your light shall break forth like the morning,
Your healing shall spring forth speedily,
And your righteousness shall go before you;
The glory of the LORD shall be your rear guard.

Isaiah 58:6-8 NKJV

Consequently, this 3D Fasting is something I have experienced
first-hand in my life over the last 25 years, especially when the Lord has
led me to go on fasts of various time periods such as 3 days, 7 days, 21
days, and even 40 days. I mention this, not to boast in any way, but
rather to share with you that fasting is a rudiment I have personally

applied to my life and have seen great results from. In fact, my personal experiences of 3D Fasting in the years of 2004, 2008, 2010, 2011, 2013, and up to this 2020 year have been a major part of what God has used to prepare, position, and posture me for in His kingdom. Collectively, these fasts have greatly helped me to move forward in the supernatural things and divine assignments God had already prepared in advance for me to prepare to advance in.

Subsequently, the result of my obedience to God's call for me to fast during those times directly impacted my life, marriage, children, ministry, and so much more. In each of these time periods of fasting, I can attest to the fact God had me abstain from the things of this world, in order to attach myself even more to the Lord, so I could also experience His accelerated work. All of these fasts resulted in God, not only moving in a supernatural accelerated manner in my life, family, and ministry, but there were specific times when certain fasts resulted in the supernatural accelerated moves of God in the lives of others such as my dear friend, Andrew Cabasa. In honoring him, allow me to mention Andrew is presently an Associate Minister of the Next Gen Ministries at Cornerstone Church led by our great mutual friend, Next Gen Director Pastor Michael Fernandez.

As for Andrew, I vividly recall shortly after the Lord graced me to complete a 40-day liquid fast from August 25th through October 3rd in 2011, that Andrew was miraculously healed of a broken foot on Wednesday, November 2, 2011. This miraculous healing occurred during one of the citywide young adult services I led at the time, together with my team, at Cornerstone Church. That night, Associate Pastor Frank Hechavarria of King Jesus Ministry in Miami, Florida led by Apostle Guillermo Maldonado, was our guest minister. As Pastor Frank ministered alongside of our worship team during a powerful time of ministry near the end of our service, Andrew's broken foot, which according to his doctor was supposed to take at least six weeks to heal, was instantly healed during the worship service. Interestingly enough, Andrew had only been wearing a cast on his foot for only two weeks. During the service, no one went to lay hands in prayer on Andrew's foot, neither did Pastor Frank nor I personally pray for Andrew from a distance. However, Andrew was miraculously healed.

Why did this happen? I wholeheartedly believe one of the major reasons why Andrew was healed was due to the 40-day fast the Lord had led me on and graced me to complete. I believe this because when our Lord Jesus Christ ended His own 40-day fast in Matthew 4, he came out of the wilderness full of the power of the Holy Spirit. Consequently and soon after, Christ began to minister with divine authority and supernatural power which resulted in miracles, signs, and wonders that produced physical healings, spiritual deliverances and much more. Hence, I believe God utilized my 40-day liquid fast to prepare, position, and posture us before Him and in His presence, so we could access the power of His Holy Spirit to release revival power into and through our lives in an accelerated manner.

Now with that in mind, I must emphasize I truly believe fasting is a rudiment for revival that can accelerate God's supernatural move in our lives beyond all we can ask or think. In fact, my life was profoundly impacted by a 31-day fast God led Pastor Matthew Hagee of Cornerstone Church to go on from January 1st through January 31st of 2008. About a year or so after his fast, Pastor Matthew shared with me that during his fast, which was approximately five months before he and I had ever met, he specifically prayed for God to bring to him the new leaders God wanted to add to Pastor Matthew's Joshua's Generation pastoral team. Making a long story short, almost four months after completing his fast, on Sunday night, May 25, 2008, God answered Pastor Matthew's prayer by utilizing Dr. Chris Hill to literally bring me to the green room of Pastor Matthew and Pastor Hagee before Dr. Hill ministered that night in their service. Many months later, Pastor Matthew shared with me how me joining his pastoral staff was a direct result of his own 31-day fast.

Now if I had more time and space, then I would share with you many other testimonials of how extended fasts can cause the effects of 3D Fasting to take place in all of our lives. However, I must continue with the rest of this chapter and share with you what God has revealed to me to be the Ten Powerful Purposes of Fasting. Yes, there are at least ten powerful purposes for fasting that can greatly impact our lives and those around us, if we choose to practice this reverent rudiment for revival.

Allow me to explain. The first two purposes, which are biblically based in Deuteronomy 9, are 1) for us to receive God's word in times of major transitions in the lives of His people including our own, and 2) for us to intercede for God's mercy to be made available to His people including our very own family members. These two purposes are evident in the experience Moses had with God, the people of Israel, and his biological brother Aaron, as can be observed in Deuteronomy 9:7-29 which says:

> [7] *Remember this and never forget how you aroused the anger of the LORD your God in the wilderness. From the day you left Egypt until you arrived here, you have been rebellious against the LORD.* [8] *At Horeb you aroused the LORD's wrath so that he was angry enough to destroy you.* [9] *When I went up on the mountain to receive the tablets of stone, the tablets of the covenant that the LORD had made with you, I stayed on the mountain forty days and forty nights; I ate no bread and drank no water.* [10] *The LORD gave me two stone tablets inscribed by the finger of God. On them were all the commandments the LORD proclaimed to you on the mountain out of the fire, on the day of the assembly.*
> [11] *At the end of the forty days and forty nights, the LORD gave me the two stone tablets, the tablets of the covenant.* [12] *Then the LORD told me, "Go down from here at once, because your people whom you brought out of Egypt have become corrupt. They have turned away quickly from what I commanded them and have made an idol for themselves."* [13] *And the LORD said to me, "I have seen this people, and they are a stiff-necked people indeed!* [14] *Let me alone, so that I may destroy them and blot out their name from under*

heaven. *And I will make you into a nation stronger and more numerous than they."*

[15] So I turned and went down from the mountain while it was ablaze with fire. And the two tablets of the covenant were in my hands. [16] When I looked, I saw that you had sinned against the LORD your God; you had made for yourselves an idol cast in the shape of a calf. You had turned aside quickly from the way that the LORD had commanded you. [17] So I took the two tablets and threw them out of my hands, breaking them to pieces before your eyes.

[18] Then once again I fell prostrate before the LORD for forty days and forty nights; I ate no bread and drank no water, because of all the sin you had committed, doing what was evil in the LORD's sight and so arousing his anger. [19] I feared the anger and wrath of the LORD, for he was angry enough with you to destroy you. But again the LORD listened to me. [20] And the LORD was angry enough with Aaron to destroy him, but at that time I prayed for Aaron too. [21] Also I took that sinful thing of yours, the calf you had made, and burned it in the fire. Then I crushed it and ground it to powder as fine as dust and threw the dust into a stream that flowed down the mountain.

[22] You also made the LORD angry at Taberah, at Massah and at Kibroth Hattaavah.

[23] And when the LORD sent you out from Kadesh Barnea, he said, "Go up and take possession of the land I have given you." But you rebelled against the command of the LORD your God. You did not trust him or obey him. [24] You have been rebellious against the LORD ever since I have known you.

[25] I lay prostrate before the LORD those forty days and forty nights because the LORD had said he would destroy you. [26] I prayed to the LORD and said, "Sovereign LORD, do not destroy your people, your own inheritance that you

*redeemed by your great power and brought out of Egypt
with a mighty hand.* [27] *Remember your servants Abraham,
Isaac and Jacob. Overlook the stubbornness of this people,
their wickedness and their sin.* [28] *Otherwise, the country
from which you brought us will say, 'Because the LORD was
not able to take them into the land he had promised them,
and because he hated them, he brought them out to put them
to death in the wilderness.'* [29] *But they are your people, your
inheritance that you brought out by your great power and
your outstretched arm."*

Deuteronomy 9:7-29 NIV

Additionally, the third purpose of fasting, which is biblically
based in 1 Kings 19, is 3) for us to pass onto our successors what God
first gave to us. This purpose of fasting can be noted in God's sovereign
succession plan and transition of the prophets Elijah and Elisha, as can
be observed in 1 Kings 19:1-21 which says:

[1] *Now Ahab told Jezebel everything Elijah had done and
how he had killed all the prophets with the sword.* [2] *So
Jezebel sent a messenger to Elijah to say, "May the gods
deal with me, be it ever so severely, if by this time tomorrow
I do not make your life like that of one of them."*
[3] *Elijah was afraid and ran for his life. When he came to
Beersheba in Judah, he left his servant there,* [4] *while he
himself went a day's journey into the wilderness. He came
to a broom bush, sat down under it and prayed that he
might die. "I have had enough, LORD," he said. "Take my
life; I am no better than my ancestors."* [5] *Then he lay down
under the bush and fell asleep.
All at once an angel touched him and said, "Get up and
eat."* [6] *He looked around, and there by his head was some
bread baked over hot coals, and a jar of water. He ate and
drank and then lay down again.*

[7] The angel of the LORD came back a second time and touched him and said, "Get up and eat, for the journey is too much for you." [8] So he got up and ate and drank. Strengthened by that food, he traveled forty days and forty nights until he reached Horeb, the mountain of God. [9] There he went into a cave and spent the night.

And the word of the LORD came to him: "What are you doing here, Elijah?"

[10] He replied, "I have been very zealous for the LORD God Almighty. The Israelites have rejected your covenant, torn down your altars, and put your prophets to death with the sword. I am the only one left, and now they are trying to kill me too."

[11] The LORD said, "Go out and stand on the mountain in the presence of the LORD, for the LORD is about to pass by."

Then a great and powerful wind tore the mountains apart and shattered the rocks before the LORD, but the LORD was not in the wind. After the wind there was an earthquake, but the LORD was not in the earthquake. [12] After the earthquake came a fire, but the LORD was not in the fire. And after the fire came a gentle whisper. [13] When Elijah heard it, he pulled his cloak over his face and went out and stood at the mouth of the cave.

Then a voice said to him, "What are you doing here, Elijah?"

[14] He replied, "I have been very zealous for the LORD God Almighty. The Israelites have rejected your covenant, torn down your altars, and put your prophets to death with the sword. I am the only one left, and now they are trying to kill me too."

[15] The LORD said to him, "Go back the way you came, and go to the Desert of Damascus. When you get there, anoint Hazael king over Aram. [16] Also, anoint Jehu son of Nimshi king over Israel, and anoint Elisha son of Shaphat from

Abel Meholah to succeed you as prophet. [17] Jehu will put to death any who escape the sword of Hazael, and Elisha will put to death any who escape the sword of Jehu. [18] Yet I reserve seven thousand in Israel—all whose knees have not bowed down to Baal and whose mouths have not kissed him."

[19] So Elijah went from there and found Elisha son of Shaphat. He was plowing with twelve yoke of oxen, and he himself was driving the twelfth pair. Elijah went up to him and threw his cloak around him. [20] Elisha then left his oxen and ran after Elijah. "Let me kiss my father and mother goodbye," he said, "and then I will come with you."
"Go back," Elijah replied. "What have I done to you?"
[21] So Elisha left him and went back. He took his yoke of oxen and slaughtered them. He burned the plowing equipment to cook the meat and gave it to the people, and they ate. Then he set out to follow Elijah and became his servant.

1 Kings 19:1-21 NIV

Likewise, the fourth, fifth, and sixth purposes for fasting, which are biblically based on Daniel 1 and Esther 4 and 5 are 4) for us to graciously obtain favor with God and humanity, 5) access heavenly intelligence and wisdom, and 6) receive a supernatural anointing which authorizes and empowers us to combat the attack of God's enemies against His people, in order to deliver God's people from wicked plots. These purposes of fasting can be seen in the intervention of the Prophet Daniel and Queen Esther during each of the crucial times they lived in, as can be observed in Daniel 1:1-21 and Esther 4:1-17; 5:1-5 which say:

[1] In the third year of the reign of Jehoiakim king of Judah, Nebuchadnezzar king of Babylon came to Jerusalem and besieged it. [2] And the Lord delivered Jehoiakim king of Judah into his hand, along with some of the articles from

the temple of God. These he carried off to the temple of his god in Babylonia and put in the treasure house of his god. ³ Then the king ordered Ashpenaz, chief of his court officials, to bring into the king's service some of the Israelites from the royal family and the nobility— ⁴ young men without any physical defect, handsome, showing aptitude for every kind of learning, well informed, quick to understand, and qualified to serve in the king's palace. He was to teach them the language and literature of the Babylonians. ⁵ The king assigned them a daily amount of food and wine from the king's table. They were to be trained for three years, and after that they were to enter the king's service.

⁶ Among those who were chosen were some from Judah: Daniel, Hananiah, Mishael and Azariah. ⁷ The chief official gave them new names: to Daniel, the name Belteshazzar; to Hananiah, Shadrach; to Mishael, Meshach; and to Azariah, Abednego.

⁸ But Daniel resolved not to defile himself with the royal food and wine, and he asked the chief official for permission not to defile himself this way. ⁹ Now God had caused the official to show favor and compassion to Daniel, ¹⁰ but the official told Daniel, "I am afraid of my lord the king, who has assigned your food and drink. Why should he see you looking worse than the other young men your age? The king would then have my head because of you."

¹¹ Daniel then said to the guard whom the chief official had appointed over Daniel, Hananiah, Mishael and Azariah, ¹² "Please test your servants for ten days: Give us nothing but vegetables to eat and water to drink. ¹³ Then compare our appearance with that of the young men who eat the royal food, and treat your servants in accordance with what you see." ¹⁴ So he agreed to this and tested them for ten days.

[15] At the end of the ten days they looked healthier and better nourished than any of the young men who ate the royal food. [16] So the guard took away their choice food and the wine they were to drink and gave them vegetables instead. [17] To these four young men God gave knowledge and understanding of all kinds of literature and learning. And Daniel could understand visions and dreams of all kinds. [18] At the end of the time set by the king to bring them into his service, the chief official presented them to Nebuchadnezzar. [19] The king talked with them, and he found none equal to Daniel, Hananiah, Mishael and Azariah; so they entered the king's service. [20] In every matter of wisdom and understanding about which the king questioned them, he found them ten times better than all the magicians and enchanters in his whole kingdom. 21 And Daniel remained there until the first year of King Cyrus.

Daniel 1:1-21 NIV

[1] When Mordecai learned of all that had been done, he tore his clothes, put on sackcloth and ashes, and went out into the city, wailing loudly and bitterly. [2] But he went only as far as the king's gate, because no one clothed in sackcloth was allowed to enter it. [3] In every province to which the edict and order of the king came, there was great mourning among the Jews, with fasting, weeping and wailing. Many lay in sackcloth and ashes.

[4] When Esther's eunuchs and female attendants came and told her about Mordecai, she was in great distress. She sent clothes for him to put on instead of his sackcloth, but he would not accept them. [5] Then Esther summoned Hathak, one of the king's eunuchs assigned to attend her, and ordered him to find out what was troubling Mordecai and why.

6 So Hathak went out to Mordecai in the open square of the city in front of the king's gate. 7 Mordecai told him everything that had happened to him, including the exact amount of money Haman had promised to pay into the royal treasury for the destruction of the Jews. 8 He also gave him a copy of the text of the edict for their annihilation, which had been published in Susa, to show to Esther and explain it to her, and he told him to instruct her to go into the king's presence to beg for mercy and plead with him for her people.

9 Hathak went back and reported to Esther what Mordecai had said. 10 Then she instructed him to say to Mordecai, 11 "All the king's officials and the people of the royal provinces know that for any man or woman who approaches the king in the inner court without being summoned the king has but one law: that they be put to death unless the king extends the gold scepter to them and spares their lives. But thirty days have passed since I was called to go to the king."

12 When Esther's words were reported to Mordecai, 13 he sent back this answer: "Do not think that because you are in the king's house you alone of all the Jews will escape. 14 For if you remain silent at this time, relief and deliverance for the Jews will arise from another place, but you and your father's family will perish. And who knows but that you have come to your royal position for such a time as this?"

15 Then Esther sent this reply to Mordecai: 16 "Go, gather together all the Jews who are in Susa, and fast for me. Do not eat or drink for three days, night or day. I and my attendants will fast as you do. When this is done, I will go to the king, even though it is against the law. And if I perish, I perish."

[17] So Mordecai went away and carried out all of Esther's instructions.

Esther 4:1-17 NIV

[1] On the third day Esther put on her royal robes and stood in the inner court of the palace, in front of the king's hall. The king was sitting on his royal throne in the hall, facing the entrance. [2] When he saw Queen Esther standing in the court, he was pleased with her and held out to her the gold scepter that was in his hand. So Esther approached and touched the tip of the scepter.

[3] Then the king asked, "What is it, Queen Esther? What is your request? Even up to half the kingdom, it will be given you."

[4] "If it pleases the king," replied Esther, "let the king, together with Haman, come today to a banquet I have prepared for him."

[5] "Bring Haman at once," the king said, "so that we may do what Esther asks."

Esther 5:1-5 NIV

Furthermore, the seventh purpose for fasting, which is biblically based on Joel 1 and 2, is 7) for God's people, beginning with the spiritual leaders, to receive His call for them to humble themselves before God, in order to replace their rightly deserved judgement with His mercifully gracious blessings and Holy Spirit outpouring. This purpose can be observed in the ministry of the Prophet Joel, as can be observed in Joel 1:13-15 and Joel 2:12-19, 28 which say:

[13] Put on sackcloth, you priests, and mourn;
*   wail, you who minister before the altar.*
Come, spend the night in sackcloth,
*   you who minister before my God;*
for the grain offerings and drink offerings

are withheld from the house of your God.
14 Declare a holy fast;
call a sacred assembly.
Summon the elders
and all who live in the land
to the house of the LORD your God,
and cry out to the LORD.
15 Alas for that day!
For the day of the LORD is near;
it will come like destruction from the Almighty.

Joel 1:13-15 NIV

12 "Even now," declares the LORD,
"return to me with all your heart,
with fasting and weeping and mourning."
13 Rend your heart
and not your garments.
Return to the LORD your God,
for he is gracious and compassionate,
slow to anger and abounding in love,
and he relents from sending calamity.
14 Who knows? He may turn and relent
and leave behind a blessing—
grain offerings and drink offerings
for the LORD your God.
15 Blow the trumpet in Zion,
declare a holy fast,
call a sacred assembly.
16 Gather the people,
consecrate the assembly;
bring together the elders,
gather the children,
those nursing at the breast.
Let the bridegroom leave his room

and the bride her chamber.
¹⁷ Let the priests, who minister before the LORD,
weep between the portico and the altar.
Let them say, "Spare your people, LORD.
Do not make your inheritance an object of scorn,
a byword among the nations.
Why should they say among the peoples,
'Where is their God?'"
¹⁸ Then the LORD was jealous for his land
and took pity on his people.
¹⁹ The LORD replied to them:
"I am sending you grain, new wine and olive oil,
enough to satisfy you fully;
never again will I make you
an object of scorn to the nations.

²⁸ "And afterward,
I will pour out my Spirit on all people.
Your sons and daughters will prophesy,
your old men will dream dreams,
your young men will see visions.

Joel 2:12-19, 28 NIV

Additionally, the eighth purpose of fasting, which is biblically based on Jonah 3, is 8) for ushering in revival to governing authorities and the people they lead in their cities and beyond. This is evident in the testimony of the prophet Jonah's ministry to the city of Nineveh, as can be observed in Jonah 3:1-10 which says:

¹ Then the word of the LORD came to Jonah a second time:
² "Go to the great city of Nineveh and proclaim to it the message I give you."
³ Jonah obeyed the word of the LORD and went to Nineveh. Now Nineveh was a very large city; it took three days to go

*through it. ⁴ Jonah began by going a day's journey into the
city, proclaiming, "Forty more days and Nineveh will be
overthrown." ⁵ The Ninevites believed God. A fast was
proclaimed, and all of them, from the greatest to the least,
put on sackcloth.
⁶ When Jonah's warning reached the king of Nineveh, he
rose from his throne, took off his royal robes, covered
himself with sackcloth and sat down in the dust. ⁷ This is the
proclamation he issued in Nineveh:
"By the decree of the king and his nobles:
Do not let people or animals, herds or flocks, taste
anything; do not let them eat or drink. ⁸ But let people and
animals be covered with sackcloth. Let everyone call
urgently on God. Let them give up their evil ways and their
violence. ⁹ Who knows? God may yet relent and with
compassion turn from his fierce anger so that we will not
perish."
¹⁰ When God saw what they did and how they turned from
their evil ways, he relented and did not bring on them the
destruction he had threatened.*

Jonah 3:1-10 NIV

Second to last, the ninth purpose of fasting, which is biblically
based on Luke 4, is 9) for launching us into Christ's kingdom ministry in
order to fulfill His Great Commission to us which can result in the
greatest harvest of souls being saved, healed, delivered, prospered, and
so much more all over the world. Of course, I believe we are about to
experience that in this 2020 year and subsequent decade at the greatest
level, dimension, and measure that has ever been experienced yet in
human history. This purpose of fasting is best exemplified in the life and
ministry of our Lord Jesus Christ, as can be observed in Luke 4:1-2, 14-
21 which says:

151

*¹ Jesus, full of the Holy Spirit, left the Jordan and was led
by the Spirit into the wilderness, ² where for forty days he
was tempted by the devil. He ate nothing during those days,
and at the end of them he was hungry.*

*¹⁴ Jesus returned to Galilee in the power of the Spirit, and
news about him spread through the whole countryside. ¹⁵ He
was teaching in their synagogues, and everyone praised
him.*
*¹⁶ He went to Nazareth, where he had been brought up, and
on the Sabbath day he went into the synagogue, as was his
custom. He stood up to read, ¹⁷ and the scroll of the prophet
Isaiah was handed to him. Unrolling it, he found the place
where it is written:*
¹⁸ "The Spirit of the Lord is on me,
    because he has anointed me
    to proclaim good news to the poor.
He has sent me to proclaim freedom for the prisoners
    and recovery of sight for the blind,
to set the oppressed free,
¹⁹   to proclaim the year of the Lord's favor."
*²⁰ Then he rolled up the scroll, gave it back to the attendant
and sat down. The eyes of everyone in the synagogue were
fastened on him. ²¹ He began by saying to them, "Today this
scripture is fulfilled in your hearing."*

Luke 4:1-2, 14-21 NIV

Lastly, the tenth purpose for fasting, which is biblically based in
Mark 9, is 10) for us to effectively administer the authority and power of
Jesus Christ and the Holy Spirit so we can cast out evil spirits from
people's lives and families which have been tormenting and trying to kill
them, as can be observed in Mark 9:14-29 which says:

[14] *When they came to the other disciples, they saw a large crowd around them and the teachers of the law arguing with them.* [15] *As soon as all the people saw Jesus, they were overwhelmed with wonder and ran to greet him.*

[16] *"What are you arguing with them about?" he asked.*

[17] *A man in the crowd answered, "Teacher, I brought you my son, who is possessed by a spirit that has robbed him of speech.* [18] *Whenever it seizes him, it throws him to the ground. He foams at the mouth, gnashes his teeth and becomes rigid. I asked your disciples to drive out the spirit, but they could not."*

[19] *"You unbelieving generation," Jesus replied, "how long shall I stay with you? How long shall I put up with you? Bring the boy to me."*

[20] *So they brought him. When the spirit saw Jesus, it immediately threw the boy into a convulsion. He fell to the ground and rolled around, foaming at the mouth.*

[21] *Jesus asked the boy's father, "How long has he been like this?"*

"From childhood," he answered. [22] *"It has often thrown him into fire or water to kill him. But if you can do anything, take pity on us and help us."*

[23] *"'If you can'?" said Jesus. "Everything is possible for one who believes."*

[24] *Immediately the boy's father exclaimed, "I do believe; help me overcome my unbelief!"*

[25] *When Jesus saw that a crowd was running to the scene, he rebuked the impure spirit. "You deaf and mute spirit," he said, "I command you, come out of him and never enter him again."*

[26] *The spirit shrieked, convulsed him violently and came out. The boy looked so much like a corpse that many said, "He's dead."* [27] *But Jesus took him by the hand and lifted him to his feet, and he stood up.*

²⁸ After Jesus had gone indoors, his disciples asked him privately, "Why couldn't we drive it out?"
²⁹ He replied, "This kind can come out only by prayer (and fasting)."

Mark 9:14-29 NIV

Now with all of these ten powerful purposes of fasting in mind, we can see how extremely empowering the reverent rudiment of fasting is and can be in our lives and in the lives of many others. Therefore, I believe that, now more than ever, we need to practice this revival rudiment. When we do, then God will utilize our fasting to release revivalists into the world according to Acts 13:1-3 which says:

¹ Now in the Church that was at Antioch there were certain prophets and teachers: Barnabas, Simeon who was called Niger, Lucius of Cyrene, Manaen who had been brought up with Herod the tetrarch, and Saul. ² As they ministered to the Lord and fasted, the Holy Spirit said, "Now separate to Me Barnabas and Saul for the work to which I have called them." ³ Then, having fasted and prayed, and laid hands on them, they sent them away.

Acts 13:1-3 NKJV

From this passage of scripture, and all of the other scriptures we have considered in this chapter, it is undeniably evident that it is God's will for us and Christ's call unto us to make sure we apply this reverent rudiment of fasting to our lives and to our service in God's kingdom on earth. When we do, God will release more of His authority and power upon us, as His church, so we can advance in what He has already prepared in advance for us. Therefore, now more than ever, we must do more fasting and less feasting, because our well-being and the well-being of others depends on it. History is in the making for the next great awakening, and our fasting in obedience to God's word will accelerate His powerful work so we can receive and release revival now!

154

CHAPTER 9
THE RUDIMENT OF WORSHIP

The third of five reverent rudiments for revival now is worship. Although the word "worship," like "fasting," does not appear in Acts 1 or 2, as it pertains to the account of the Apostle Peter and the 120 disciples, a closer look into the Jewish Feast of Pentecost, can reveal how worship is very much connected to revival. The biblical basis for this connection is registered in Leviticus 23:15-22 and supported in Exodus 34, Deuteronomy 16, and Numbers 28. In these passages of scripture, the Feast of Pentecost, also known as the Feast of Weeks or Shavuot, which refers to seven weeks after the first Feast of Passover, is noted as a feast during which the Jews were required to ascend to the temple of God in Jerusalem. Upon their arrival from all over the surrounding regions, they were to bring their latter Spring harvest first fruit of their wheat grain offering, along with wheat leavened bread wave offerings, to the God of Israel. This was done as an act of worship. Hence, this reveals the connection of worship to the Feast of Pentecost and to the revival that occurred in Acts 2. This can be further understood when we consider the following scriptures from Leviticus 23:15-22, Exodus 34:22, Deuteronomy 16:9-10, and Numbers 28:26 which say:

155

[15] And you shall count for yourselves from the day after the Sabbath, from the day that you brought the sheaf of the wave offering: seven Sabbaths shall be completed. [16] Count fifty days to the day after the seventh Sabbath; then you shall offer a new grain offering to the LORD. [17] You shall bring from your dwellings two wave loaves of two-tenths of an ephah. They shall be of fine flour; they shall be baked with leaven. They are the firstfruits to the LORD. [18] And you shall offer with the bread seven lambs of the first year, without blemish, one young bull, and two rams. They shall be as a burnt offering to the LORD, with their grain offering and their drink offerings, an offering made by fire for a sweet aroma to the LORD. [19] Then you shall sacrifice one kid of the goats as a sin offering, and two male lambs of the first year as a sacrifice of a peace offering. [20] The priest shall wave them with the bread of the firstfruits as a wave offering before the LORD, with the two lambs. They shall be holy to the LORD for the priest. [21] And you shall proclaim on the same day that it is a holy convocation to you. You shall do no customary work on it. It shall be a statute forever in all your dwellings throughout your generations.

[22] 'When you reap the harvest of your land, you shall not wholly reap the corners of your field when you reap, nor shall you gather any gleaning from your harvest. You shall leave them for the poor and for the stranger: I am the LORD your God.

Leviticus 23:15-22 NKJV

[22] And you shall observe the Feast of Weeks, of the firstfruits of wheat harvest, and the Feast of Ingathering at the year's end.

Exodus 34:22 NKJV

⁹ You shall count seven weeks for yourself; begin to count the seven weeks from the time you begin to put the sickle to the grain. ¹⁰ Then you shall keep the Feast of Weeks to the LORD your God with the tribute of a freewill offering from your hand, which you shall give as the LORD your God blesses you.

Deuteronomy 16:9-10 NKJV

²⁶ Also on the day of the firstfruits, when you bring a new grain offering to the LORD at your Feast of Weeks, you shall have a holy convocation. You shall do no customary work.

Numbers 28:26 NKJV

Consequently, the Apostle Peter and the 120 disciples, who were all Jewish, would have been observing this feast and bringing the same kind of offerings or worship established in the original Feast of Pentecost in the Old Testament. Thus, the giving of offerings, also known as a form of worship, would have been a required reverent rudiment for the revival they experienced on the Day of Pentecost in the New Testament. Yet before we assume what worship is, and understandably associate it with the great songs, music, melodies, harmonies, and song set-lists we love and have on our various electronic devices, it is very important we consider the first time the word "worship" appears in God's word. In doing so, we can discover what its first mention reveals to us about worship. With that in mind let us consider Genesis 22:1-19 where worship is first mentioned in the Bible.

¹ Now it came to pass after these things that God tested Abraham, and said to him, "Abraham!"
And he said, "Here I am."
² Then He said, "Take now your son, your only son Isaac, whom you love, and go to the land of Moriah, and offer him there as a burnt offering on one of the mountains of which I shall tell you."

3 So Abraham rose early in the morning and saddled his donkey, and took two of his young men with him, and Isaac his son; and he split the wood for the burnt offering, and arose and went to the place of which God had told him.
4 Then on the third day Abraham lifted his eyes and saw the place afar off. 5 And Abraham said to his young men, "Stay here with the donkey; the lad and I will go yonder and worship, and we will come back to you."
6 So Abraham took the wood of the burnt offering and laid it on Isaac his son; and he took the fire in his hand, and a knife, and the two of them went together. 7 But Isaac spoke to Abraham his father and said, "My father!"
And he said, "Here I am, my son."
Then he said, "Look, the fire and the wood, but where is the lamb for a burnt offering?"
8 And Abraham said, "My son, God will provide for Himself the lamb for a burnt offering." So the two of them went together.
9 Then they came to the place of which God had told him. And Abraham built an altar there and placed the wood in order; and he bound Isaac his son and laid him on the altar, upon the wood. 10 And Abraham stretched out his hand and took the knife to slay his son.
11 But the Angel of the LORD called to him from heaven and said, "Abraham, Abraham!"
So he said, "Here I am."
12 And He said, "Do not lay your hand on the lad, or do anything to him; for now I know that you fear God, since you have not withheld your son, your only son, from Me."
13 Then Abraham lifted his eyes and looked, and there behind him was a ram caught in a thicket by its horns. So Abraham went and took the ram, and offered it up for a burnt offering instead of his son. 14 And Abraham called the

name of the place, The-LORD-Will-Provide; as it is said to this day, "In the Mount of the LORD it shall be provided." [15] Then the Angel of the LORD called to Abraham a second time out of heaven, [16] and said: "By Myself I have sworn, says the LORD, because you have done this thing, and have not withheld your son, your only son— [17] blessing I will bless you, and multiplying I will multiply your descendants as the stars of the heaven and as the sand which is on the seashore; and your descendants shall possess the gate of their enemies. [18] In your seed all the nations of the earth shall be blessed, because you have obeyed My voice." [19] So Abraham returned to his young men, and they rose and went together to Beersheba; and Abraham dwelt at Beersheba.

Genesis 22:1-19 NKJV

In this passage, we find the first appearance of worship in the scriptures, and shockingly enough, there is no singing, instrument playing, worship teams or choir participation occurring. Instead what we find is God calling Abraham to take his son of promise, Isaac, to an altar of sacrificial obedience. This, therefore, is the original and initial act of worship registered in the Bible. Correspondingly, the end result of Abraham's worship was God figuratively reviving or restoring the life of Isaac, because of Abraham's lifestyle of genuine and original worship.

As for this authentic and initial kind of worship, interestingly enough, we should note that the word origin of "worship" comes from two words which are "worth" and "ship." While the word "worth" speaks to the importance of the great value of something, the word "ship" speaks to the importance of the great size of something. Additionally, when both of these words are united to form "worth-ship" or "worship," these words reveal that authentic worship is actually the act of us offering to God something that is both of great value and great size in our lives. So why should we worship, in addition to knowing that our God is great and greatly to be praised according to Psalm 145:3 which says?

³ Great is the LORD, and greatly to be praised;
And His greatness is unsearchable.

Psalm 145:3 NKJV

According to 2 Chronicles 5 and 7, worship attracts God's presence and glory to those who worship Him. This can be clearly seen in 2 Chronicles, when the first temple of God is dedicated to Him in worship, and He subsequently responds to worship with His presence and glory manifesting as a cloud by day and a column of fire by night, as described in 2 Chronicles 5:13-14 and 7:1-5 which say:

¹³ indeed it came to pass, when the trumpeters and singers were as one, to make one sound to be heard in praising and thanking the LORD, and when they lifted up their voice with the trumpets and cymbals and instruments of music, and praised the LORD, saying:
"For He is good,
For His mercy endures forever,"
that the house, the house of the LORD, was filled with a cloud, ¹⁴ so that the priests could not continue ministering because of the cloud; for the glory of the LORD filled the house of God.

2 Chronicles 5:13-14 NKJV

¹ When Solomon had finished praying, fire came down from heaven and consumed the burnt offering and the sacrifices; and the glory of the LORD filled the temple. ² And the priests could not enter the house of the LORD, because the glory of the LORD had filled the LORD's house. ³ When all the children of Israel saw how the fire came down, and the glory of the LORD on the temple, they bowed their faces to the ground on the pavement, and worshiped and praised the LORD, saying:

"For He is good,
For His mercy endures forever."
⁴ Then the king and all the people offered sacrifices before
the LORD. ⁵ King Solomon offered a sacrifice of twenty-two
thousand bulls and one hundred and twenty thousand sheep.
So the king and all the people dedicated the house of God.

2 Chronicles 7:1-5 NKJV

Now when we consider these passages of scripture, we can better understand why, in the New Testament, God calls His people through the Apostle Paul to live their lives as a living sacrifice, which is their true and proper act of worship unto the Lord, according to Romans 12:1 which says:

¹ Therefore, I urge you, brothers and sisters, in view of
God's mercy, to offer your bodies as a living sacrifice, holy
and pleasing to God—this is your true and proper worship.

Romans 12:1 NKJV

Additionally, we can see how our Lord Jesus Christ shared this divine call to worship with the Samaritan woman in John 4, and Mary, the sister of Lazarus, in John 11. In John 4:23-24, Jesus tells the Samaritan woman the following:

²³ But the hour is coming, and now is, when the true
worshipers will worship the Father in spirit and truth; for
the Father is seeking such to worship Him. ²⁴ God is Spirit,
and those who worship Him must worship in spirit and
truth.

John 4:23-24 NKJV

Interestingly enough, the Samaritan woman, who revealed her desire to worship God in her conversation with Jesus Christ, thereafter, experienced her personal revival which then resulted in the corporate revival of the people of her city.

Correspondingly, when we observe the lifestyle of worship in the life of Mary, the sister of Lazarus, we see something just as powerful, if not even more powerful. To better understand this, let us consider John 11:1-5, 38-45 which says:

> *[1] Now a man named Lazarus was sick. He was from Bethany, the village of Mary and her sister Martha. [2] (This Mary, whose brother Lazarus now lay sick, was the same one who poured perfume on the Lord and wiped his feet with her hair.) [3] So the sisters sent word to Jesus, "Lord, the one you love is sick."*
> *[4] When he heard this, Jesus said, "This sickness will not end in death. No, it is for God's glory so that God's Son may be glorified through it." [5] Now Jesus loved Martha and her sister and Lazarus.*
>
> *[38] Jesus, once more deeply moved, came to the tomb. It was a cave with a stone laid across the entrance. [39] "Take away the stone," he said.*
> *"But, Lord," said Martha, the sister of the dead man, "by this time there is a bad odor, for he has been there four days."*
> *[40] Then Jesus said, "Did I not tell you that if you believe, you will see the glory of God?"*
> *[41] So they took away the stone. Then Jesus looked up and said, "Father, I thank you that you have heard me. [42] I knew that you always hear me, but I said this for the benefit of the people standing here, that they may believe that you sent me."*
> *[43] When he had said this, Jesus called in a loud voice, "Lazarus, come out!" [44] The dead man came out, his hands*

*and feet wrapped with strips of linen, and a cloth around
his face.*

*Jesus said to them, "Take off the grave clothes and let him
go."*

*[45] Therefore many of the Jews who had come to visit Mary,
and had seen what Jesus did, believed in him.*

John 11:1-5, 38-45 NIV

Through this passage of scripture, we can see that Mary,
Lazarus' sister, who was a true worshipper, provoked Jesus Christ,
through her worship, to literally revive her brother Lazarus from the dead
even after her brother had been dead for four days. Now for the sake of
further emphasizing and better understanding this point, I believe it
would be very helpful for us to observe the difference between Mary and
her sister Martha, as registered in John 11:17-37 which says:

*[17] On his arrival, Jesus found that Lazarus had already been
in the tomb for four days. [18] Now Bethany was less than two
miles from Jerusalem, [19] and many Jews had come to
Martha and Mary to comfort them in the loss of their
brother. [20] When Martha heard that Jesus was coming, she
went out to meet him, but Mary stayed at home.*

*[21] "Lord," Martha said to Jesus, "if you had been here, my
brother would not have died. [22] But I know that even now
God will give you whatever you ask."*

[23] Jesus said to her, "Your brother will rise again."

*[24] Martha answered, "I know he will rise again in the
resurrection at the last day."*

*[25] Jesus said to her, "I am the resurrection and the life. The
one who believes in me will live, even though they die;*

*[26] and whoever lives by believing in me will never die. Do
you believe this?"*

*[27] "Yes, Lord," she replied, "I believe that you are the
Messiah, the Son of God, who is to come into the world."*

28 After she had said this, she went back and called her sister Mary aside. "The Teacher is here," she said, "and is asking for you." 29 When Mary heard this, she got up quickly and went to him. 30 Now Jesus had not yet entered the village, but was still at the place where Martha had met him. 31 When the Jews who had been with Mary in the house, comforting her, noticed how quickly she got up and went out, they followed her, supposing she was going to the tomb to mourn there.

32 When Mary reached the place where Jesus was and saw him, she fell at his feet and said, "Lord, if you had been here, my brother would not have died."

33 When Jesus saw her weeping, and the Jews who had come along with her also weeping, he was deeply moved in spirit and troubled. 34 "Where have you laid him?" he asked.

"Come and see, Lord," they replied.

35 Jesus wept.

36 Then the Jews said, "See how he loved him!"

37 But some of them said, "Could not he who opened the eyes of the blind man have kept this man from dying?"

John 11:17-37 NKJV

This is truly a revealing passage of scripture. Why? Interestingly enough, Martha's name means "lady-like," while Mary's name means "rebellious." Yet Martha's encounter with Jesus Christ was more about her knowledge of theology and eschatology than anything else. Meanwhile, Mary's encounter with Jesus Christ was more about her relationally knowing and accessing the power of heaven in her present time, instead of only doing so in the distant far off end-time future.

Additionally, although on a prior occasion in Luke 10, Martha had displayed the great act of welcoming Jesus Christ into their home, she then quickly became distracted and got worried about her house work and whined to Jesus about her sister Mary not helping her out around the house. All the while, after Jesus was welcomed into their home, Mary instead, 1) went straight to Him, 2) sat at His feet, 3) listened to Him, and 4) invested her time in being with Jesus, without letting her sister distract her. This is clearly evident in Luke 10:32-42 which says:

> *[38] Now it happened as they went that He entered a certain village; and a certain woman named Martha welcomed Him into her house. [39] And she had a sister called Mary, who also sat at Jesus' feet and heard His word. [40] But Martha was distracted with much serving, and she approached Him and said, "Lord, do You not care that my sister has left me to serve alone? Therefore tell her to help me."*
> *[41] And Jesus answered and said to her, "Martha, Martha, you are worried and troubled about many things. [42] But one thing is needed, and Mary has chosen that good part, which will not be taken away from her."*
>
> Luke 10:38-42 NKJV

Now when we connect this distinction between Mary and Martha to John 11, we can recall that Martha and Mary had met Jesus Christ at separate times, but in the same place where they said the same statement to Him about their dead brother Lazarus. However, Christ responded differently to each of them. In fact, He favored Mary's worshipful and relationally based approach towards Him, far beyond Martha's whining and religiously based approach. Why? While Martha had a lot of theologically informed head-knowledge about Jesus Christ, the kingdom of God, and end-time studies, Mary had a wholehearted intimate pursuit of knowing Jesus Christ personally, entering into His kingdom relationally, and faithfully trusting in Him. In fact, Mary's intimate worshipful expression demonstrated she believed that if Jesus Christ could resurrect believers in the end-times, then He could also resurrect her brother Lazarus in her present time.

Interestingly enough, of the two sisters, only Mary is registered in John 11 and 12, as being the one who anointed Jesus Christ's feet with a very expensive fragrant oil which Bible scholars estimate was valued at one year's salary during the time of Lazarus. Furthermore, Mary even wiped Jesus' feet with her very own hair. Why is this extremely important to make note of? The answer is because it was Mary's lifestyle of extravagant worship that provoked Jesus Christ to resurrect and revive her dead brother Lazarus.

Evidence of this can be found in John 11:41-43, when Jesus Christ Himself, before resurrecting Lazarus, takes time to look up to His Heavenly Father and give Him thanks. When Jesus does so, thereafter, He mentions He was giving thanks to His Heavenly Father so those who were observing the situation could notice Him doing so. I believe the reason for this was because Jesus wanted everyone on the scene to realize how this act of gratitude, which was indeed an act of worship on His part, could provoke the revival power of God to be released on any situation including that of a dead man needing to be revived.

Correspondingly, this reminds me of a similar experience I was graced to be part of in October of 2013 regarding one of my dear friends, Pastor Josue Holguin, who is also a board member of De Jesus Ministries, together with his dear wife, Benita Holguin. Although I lived in San Antonio, Texas at the time, from Friday, October 11th through Sunday, October 13th, I was ministering evangelistically in Phoenix, Arizona. While I was there, I found out Josue, due to becoming gravely ill, had been admitted to the ICU of Laredo Medical Center in Laredo, Texas on Sunday, October 13th. While in the hospital, Josue was diagnosed with pancreatitis. Due to this serious illness, he had multiple complications which included kidney failure, pneumonia, tachycardia, and diabetes. At one point, he was only given a 2% survival rate. Obviously, his situation was very grave, to say the least. Meanwhile, I was in Phoenix having preached revival messages, including one based on the resurrection of Lazarus and its connection to a lifestyle of worship. So when the time arrived for me to return home on Tuesday, October 15th, the Lord spoke to my spirit during my flight back to San Antonio and impressed upon my heart a divine assignment. He let me know when I landed, I needed to drive past the highway exit towards my home and drive straight to Laredo. My assignment was to get to Josue and simply thank God, like Jesus' did, and pray for Josue's physical revival of health.

So I let Mildred know, received her blessing to go, obeyed our Lord, and did my part. Long story short, I arrived to the hospital, went with Benita to see Josue in the ICU room, I read out portions of John 11 over Josue's life while he was sedated, and prayed with thanksgiving and worship, together with Benita. Ultimately, I simply joined my worship and prayer with her, their families, friends, and other ministers. Our Heavenly Father was more than faithful to do His part for Josue. Within four days, Josue was taken out of ICU. Within nine days, he was back at home on track to a full recovery. To God's glory, it was a revival miracle.

Fast forward to this 2020 year, Josue no longer has any of those health issues he was diagnosed with seven years ago. In fact, he does not even need to take any of the medications he once had to take for his prior medical condition. What happened? Josue experienced a miraculous revival and restoration of health that our Heavenly Father released upon him, because worship can provoke God's greater glory to show up and raise up His people from dire straits of sickness to a miraculously healed state of being.

Therefore, because our God is no respecter of persons, I wholeheartedly believe your worship can also provoke His revival power to be released to you and through you to those around you. All you have to do is decide daily to intimately worship Jesus Christ in spirit and in truth, regardless of what sick or deathly circumstances, situations, and conditions you or your loved ones may be facing at this time. History is in the making for the next great awakening, and God wants to utilize our intimate worship to provoke His life-restoring power which can release in others revival now!

CHAPTER 10
THE RUDIMENT OF
LIVING ACCORDING TO GOD'S WORD

     The fourth of five reverent rudiments for revival now is living according to God's word. This rudiment is biblically based on Acts 1:15-20 and Acts 2:16-21, in addition to many other passages of scripture I will share in this chapter. Consider the following:

> [15] *And in those days Peter stood up in the midst of the disciples (altogether the number of names was about a hundred and twenty), and said,* [16] *"Men and brethren, this Scripture had to be fulfilled, which the Holy Spirit spoke before by the mouth of David concerning Judas, who became a guide to those who arrested Jesus;* [17] *for he was numbered with us and obtained a part in this ministry."* [18] *(Now this man purchased a field with the wages of iniquity; and falling headlong, he burst open in the middle and all his entrails gushed out.* [19] *And it became known to*

all those dwelling in Jerusalem; so that field is called in
their own language, Akel Dama, that is, Field of Blood.)
[20] *"For it is written in the Book of Psalms:*
'Let his dwelling place be desolate,
And let no one live in it';
and,
'Let another take his office.'

Acts 1:15-20 NKJV

[16] *But this is what was spoken by the Prophet Joel:*
[17] *'And it shall come to pass in the last days, says God,*
That I will pour out of My Spirit on all flesh;
Your sons and your daughters shall prophesy,
Your young men shall see visions,
Your old men shall dream dreams.
[18] *And on My menservants and on My maidservants*
I will pour out My Spirit in those days;
And they shall prophesy.
[19] *I will show wonders in heaven above*
And signs in the earth beneath:
Blood and fire and vapor of smoke.
[20] *The sun shall be turned into darkness,*
And the moon into blood,
Before the coming of the great and awesome day of the
LORD.
[21] *And it shall come to pass*
That whoever calls on the name of the LORD
Shall be saved.'

Acts 2:16-21 NKJV

In these passages of scripture, we can discover that the Apostle Peter, together with the 120 disciples who went with him to the upper room, made certain that living according to God's word and making decisions based on God's word was a priority for them. In fact, they did so in the days leading up to the Day of Pentecost and on the Day of Pentecost itself. Moreover, Peter and the other eleven apostles stood up on the Day of Pentecost and utilized God's word in Joel 2 to explain what was happening on that day. Why did this happen? I wholeheartedly believe it was because they fully understood that living according to God's word is a required reverent rudiment for revival. Furthermore, if we were to consider the rest of Acts 2 and its subsequent chapters, we would see how Peter and the other apostles regularly quoted or referenced the Old Testament scriptures, in a very similar way Jesus Christ did so during His earthly ministry.

Additional passages of God's word prove just how extremely imperative living according to God's word is in order for there to be revival in our lives. The fact is that the word of God has life and is able to revive, as registered in Psalm 119:29, 107 which says:

> *[25] My soul clings to the dust;*
> *Revive me according to Your word.*

> *[107] I am afflicted very much;*
> *Revive me, O LORD, according to Your word.*
>> *Psalm 119:25, 107 NKJV*

Correspondingly, this is indeed the case because the word of God itself is spirit and life, according to the very words of our Lord Jesus Christ, who in John 6:63 said the following:

> *[63] It is the Spirit who gives life; the flesh profits nothing. The words that I speak to you are spirit, and they are life.*
>> *John 6:63 NKJV*

Moreover, Jesus Christ reveals to us that the word of God is what we are to live and be sustained by, according to Matthew 4:4 which says:

[4]But He answered and said, "It is written, 'Man shall not live by bread alone, but by every word that proceeds from the mouth of God.' "

Matthew 4:4 NKJV

One of the many reasons this is clearly the case is because the word of God is living and active, according to Hebrews 4:12, and it is God-breathed, according to 2 Timothy 3:16-17, which respectively say:

[12]For the word of God is living and powerful, and sharper than any two-edged sword, piercing even to the division of soul and spirit, and of joints and marrow, and is a discerner of the thoughts and intents of the heart.

Hebrews 4:12 NKJV

[16]All Scripture is given by inspiration of God, and is profitable for doctrine, for reproof, for correction, for instruction in righteousness, [17]that the man of God may be complete, thoroughly equipped for every good work.

2 Timothy 3:16-17 NKJV

As a result, the word of God is so alive, Spirit-filled, and powerful that it can even revive dead situations in our lives as revealed in Acts 20:7-12 which says:

[7]Now on the first day of the week, when the disciples came together to break bread, Paul, ready to depart the next day, spoke to them and continued his message until midnight. [8]There were many lamps in the upper room where they were gathered together. [9]And in a window sat a certain young man named Eutychus, who was sinking into a deep sleep. He was overcome by sleep; and as Paul continued speaking, he fell down from the third story and was taken up dead. [10]But Paul went down, fell on him, and embracing

him said, "Do not trouble yourselves, for his life is in him."
[11] Now when he had come up, had broken bread and eaten,
and talked a long while, even till daybreak, he departed.
[12] And they brought the young man in alive, and they were
not a little comforted.

Acts 20:7-12 NKJV

In this particular passage, we see the Apostle Paul was so
devoted to the word of God, even though a young man 1) fell asleep
during Paul's message, 2) fell from the third story of the building he was
in, and 3) fell to his death. Yet, instead of being thrown off of his focus
on God's word, Paul, who lived according to God's word and understood
the reviving power of His word, used his faith in God and His word to 1)
revive the dead young man, 2) raise him up to life again, and 3) return
him to his family and friends. Now that is a real revival preaching and
illustrated message with revival power. Therefore, I believe God wants
us to become a people who are revived by His word, so we can
subsequently become a people who are known for being an expression of
God's Spirit-filled, living, active, and reviving word. This is one of the
many reasons why God inspired the Apostle Paul to write what he shared
in 2 Corinthians 3:1-3 which says:

[1] Do we begin again to commend ourselves? Or do we need,
as some others, epistles of commendation to you or letters
of commendation from you? [2] You are our epistle written in
our hearts, known and read by all men; [3] clearly you are an
epistle of Christ, ministered by us, written not with ink but
by the Spirit of the living God, not on tablets of stone but on
tablets of flesh, that is, of the heart.

2 Corinthians 3:1-3 NKJV

In fact, I believe God desires for us to become revived and living
epistles to be known and read by all, so we can testify, all the more,
about who Jesus Christ is in our lives according to His word in us.

173

Therefore, the question is, in this 2020-year of 20/20 vision, how do we really view God's word in our personal lives, and consequently, how will we treat God's word in this year and new decade?

This reminds me of a personal experience I had on Friday night, May 16, 2014 in Houston, TX, before preaching for my dear friend, Pastor Matthew Bismark, of the Global Force Young Adult Ministry at Christian Tabernacle led by Bishop Richard Heard. While leaving the hotel with my dear brother and young adult ministry leader at the time, Cesar Navarrete, the Spirit of the Lord internally spoke to my spirit. He told me "My people believe, biblically-speaking, I am the 'Word of God.' Yet, they do not treat My word as their God." When I heard this in my spirit, I must admit it caught me of guard to a certain degree. Although I was coming out of a time of prayer in preparation to minister that night, I did not expect for the Lord to speak those words to me. But I sure am glad He did. All of a sudden, to help me understand what the Lord spoke to me, I sensed Him download into my mind, heart, soul, and spirit a divine understanding of several Bible passages that I was already familiar with, but had not seen before in the way the Lord revealed them to me in that moment. The Lord reminded me of John 1:1, Revelation 19:13, and Luke 8:4-15 which say:

> [1] *In the beginning was the Word, and the Word was with God, and the Word was God.*
>
> *John 1:1 NKJV*

> [13] *He was clothed with a robe dipped in blood, and His name is called The Word of God.*
>
> *Revelation 19:13 NKJV*

> [4] *While a large crowd was gathering and people were coming to Jesus from town after town, he told this parable:* [5] *"A farmer went out to sow his seed. As he was scattering the seed, some fell along the path; it was trampled on, and the birds ate it up.* [6] *Some fell on rocky ground, and when it*

came up, the plants withered because they had no moisture.
*⁷ Other seed fell among thorns, which grew up with it and
choked the plants. ⁸ Still other seed fell on good soil. It came
up and yielded a crop, a hundred times more than was
sown."*
*When he said this, he called out, "Whoever has ears to
hear, let them hear."*
*⁹ His disciples asked him what this parable meant. ¹⁰ He
said, "The knowledge of the secrets of the kingdom of God
has been given to you, but to others I speak in parables, so
that,*

"'though seeing, they may not see;
  though hearing, they may not understand.'
*¹¹ "This is the meaning of the parable: The seed is the word
of God. ¹² Those along the path are the ones who hear, and
then the devil comes and takes away the word from their
hearts, so that they may not believe and be saved. ¹³ Those
on the rocky ground are the ones who receive the word with
joy when they hear it, but they have no root. They believe
for a while, but in the time of testing they fall away. ¹⁴ The
seed that fell among thorns stands for those who hear, but
as they go on their way they are choked by life's worries,
riches and pleasures, and they do not mature. ¹⁵ But the
seed on good soil stands for those with a noble and good
heart, who hear the word, retain it, and by persevering
produce a crop.*

Luke 8:4-15 NKJV

Through John 1:1 and Revelation 19:13, the Holy Spirit
reminded me Jesus Christ is the Word of God and that one of His biblical
names is actually the Word of God. Therefore, He reminded me the
Word of God is literally one of His names and that it is also a major part
of His identity, in addition to what God says to humanity. Then in Luke
8:4-15, which is the Parable of the Sower also registered in Mathew

13:1-23 and Mark 4:1-20, He reminded me about this parable and how the seed in this parable is His word. Correspondingly, the Lord reminded me that the different types of grounds He sows His word into represents the various ways our humanity treats His word.

Some seeds fell on the wayside, which was then eaten by the birds, representing the devil stealing the word from us. While other seeds fell on stony places, which was a shallow ground representing when the word is not able to take root in us and instead gets burned up by the scorching heat of this world. Still other seeds fell among thorns, which were choked by those thorns representing the cares of this world. However, there was other seeds that fell on good ground, which represents those of us who receive God's word, believe it, and then bear fruit of it up to a hundredfold.

From this Parable of the Sower, God showed me that how we treat His word will determine how He, as the Word of God, will treat us. Then He blew my mind when He opened my spiritual eyes to see that this parable is not only about how we as humanity treat the word of God which He speaks to us. This parable is also about how we as humanity treat His Son who is His Seed, the Word of God, sown into us. Ultimately, it is God's desire that we receive His Son, who is His Word and His Seed, so we can produce fruit for Him up to a hundredfold of harvested souls. When we do so, then He will reward our faith in Him and His Word and pour out His bountiful blessings upon us.

Once I fully processed this profound insight, I then found myself asking several questions: "How are we treating God's Word, not just in what He says, but also in who He is in us?" "Are we treating Him like one of the first three types of grounds in the parable of the sower?" "Or are we treating God's Word, Jesus Christ who is the Word of God, like the fourth ground in the parable?" "How much do we desire the Word of God, both as who He is and what He says?" Lastly, "Do we desire the Word of God like Job did which was more than His necessary food, according to Job 23:12?"

¹² I have not departed from the commandment of His lips;
I have treasured the words of His mouth
More than my necessary food.

Job 23:12 NKJV

Now with all the questions I just asked and the Bible passages we have considered so far in this chapter, I believe it is time for us to desire the Word of God, as who He is and what He says, now more than ever before. In fact, in this high-tech smart-phone era we now live in, what if we were to focus more on reading and responding to God's text, His word, more than we focus on reading and responding to everyone else's texts? Also, in this high-tech social media era we currently live in, what if we were to spend more time with our faces in God's book, than the time we spend on Facebook? Additionally, what if we were to be more engaged with the accounts or gospels of our Savior's message, which is His word, than we are engaged with our social media accounts, which is so wrapped up in our world? Lastly, what if we were to invest much more time on our face before the Lord, than we do FaceTiming our family and friends more and more?

Now please do not misunderstand me. Just like many people, I thoroughly enjoy using smart phones, social media, video-messaging technology, and other modern modes of communication we have in our world today. Yet, although I do have several social media accounts on multiple social media platforms and I also certainly see how they can be helpful to me in communicating the glorious gospel message of our Lord Jesus Christ and His Kingdom to the world, at the same time, I must plead with all of us to make sure we focus all the more on the word of God. In fact, I implore, all the more, that we make God's word the priority of our attention, affection, and adherence. We must make sure we are liking, loving, commenting on, and sharing God's word and our Savior's message, more than we do those very things with everyone else's social media messages and posts.

After all, according to Matthew 5:18, Matthew 24:35, and 1 Peter 1:23-15, the word of God will far outlast everything in the world we live in, as clearly communicated in the following passages of scriptures:

> [18] *For assuredly, I say to you, till heaven and earth pass away, one jot or one tittle will by no means pass from the law till all is fulfilled.*
>
> *Matthew 5:18 NKJV*

> [35] *Heaven and earth will pass away, but My words will by no means pass away.*
>
> *Matthew 24:35 NKJV*

> [22] *Since you have purified your souls in obeying the truth through the Spirit in sincere love of the brethren, love one another fervently with a pure heart,* [23] *having been born again, not of corruptible seed but incorruptible, through the word of God which lives and abides forever,* [24] *because*
> *"All flesh is as grass,*
> *And all the glory of man as the flower of the grass.*
> *The grass withers,*
> *And its flower falls away,*
> [25] *But the word of the LORD endures forever."*
> *Now this is the word which by the gospel was preached to you.*
>
> *1 Peter 1:22-25 NKJV*

Now when I think about the reviving and restoring power of the Word of God, as it pertains to both who He is and what He says, I recall how God used His word through my life to release supernatural healing into the lives of two young men in 2011 and 2013. The first young man was Christen DeAlejandro in Prescott, Arizona in November of 2011. The second young man was Jonathan Maldonado, who is actually my second cousin, in Rochester, New York in September of 2013. At those respective times and places, both of these young men were attending a youth camp and youth rally, while having broken bones in their feet due to high school football injuries they had suffered. Although they both had casts on their feet they were supposed to wear for at least six weeks, and although both of them were told by their doctors that surgery might be needed, when I prayed for each of them, the Lord prompted me to simply declare His word over their broken feet. So I did, and God's word took care of the rest. Making a long story short, they were both miraculously healed by God's reviving and restoring word. Interestingly enough, Christen was healed at an altar call during a youth camp, and Jonathan was healed at his home after a youth rally.

Why am I making this distinction? Because God's word is not limited to working only at church services or during youth or young adult rallies and special events. On the contrary, God's word is unlimited and will work with revival and restoring power wherever we as His people dare to believe Him to do so. In fact, I believe that now more than ever, God desires for His people to live according to His word, make decisions according to His word, and have great expectations from His word, so they can join God in utilizing His word to release revival and restorative power into the lives of many who need to be healed, delivered, saved, and so much more.

Therefore, I finish this chapter encouraging you to get ready to get much deeper into the word of God, as you allow the word of God to get much deeper into you. As this happens, Jesus Christ who is and has the Word of God, will revive you and others through you because you have intentionally decided to live according to God's word. Soon you will be testifying to your family, friends, and even strangers about the reviving and restorative powerful word of God. So be encouraged. History is in the making for the next great awakening, and your life in God's word, together with God's word in your life, will release revival now to you and through you!

CHAPTER 11
THE RUDIMENT OF UNITY

The fifth and final reverent rudiment for revival is unity. Amidst the ever increasing and rising racial tensions being experienced and expressed throughout our nation and beyond, this rudiment is especially of extraordinary importance in the world we live in today. Its primary biblical basis, within the context of the revival that occurred at the beginning of the book of Acts, is found in Acts 1:12-14 and Acts 2:1, in addition to many other passages of scripture I will share in this chapter. Consider the following:

> *[12] Then they returned to Jerusalem from the mount called Olivet, which is near Jerusalem, a Sabbath day's journey. [13] And when they had entered, they went up into the upper room where they were staying: Peter, James, John, and Andrew; Philip and Thomas; Bartholomew and Matthew; James the son of Alphaeus and Simon the Zealot; and Judas the son of James. [14] These all continued with one accord in prayer and supplication, with the women and Mary the mother of Jesus, and with His brothers.*

Acts 1:12-14 NKJV

¹ When the Day of Pentecost had fully come, they were all
with one accord in one place.

Acts 2:1 NKJV

In these passages of scripture, the first and last thing the Apostle Peter and the 120 disciples, who went to the upper room as directed by Jesus Christ, were doing before the Holy Spirit was poured out upon them on the Day of Pentecost was gathering together in unity. Correspondingly, in addition to what we can observe about them in Acts 1 and 2 regarding unity, additional passages of God's word prove just how extremely imperative unity is for revival.

To begin with, let us consider Psalm 133:1-3 which says:

¹ Behold, how good and how pleasant it is
For brethren to dwell together in unity!
² It is like the precious oil upon the head,
Running down on the beard,
The beard of Aaron,
Running down on the edge of his garments.
³ It is like the dew of Hermon,
Descending upon the mountains of Zion;
For there the LORD commanded the blessing—
Life forevermore.

Psalm 133:1-3 NKJV

In this passage, the Psalmist David reveals to us that unity provokes God's life-giving blessing from top to bottom, from north to south, and from a leader to a people. Subsequently, the Apostle Paul in Ephesians 4:1-6 and 1 Corinthians 12:12-27 has much to say about the paramount importance of unity. Consider the following:

¹ I, therefore, the prisoner of the Lord, beseech you to walk worthy of the calling with which you were called, ² with all lowliness and gentleness, with longsuffering, bearing with one another in love, ³ endeavoring to keep the unity of the Spirit in the bond of peace. ⁴ There is one body and one Spirit, just as you were called in one hope of your calling; ⁵ one Lord, one faith, one baptism; ⁶ one God and Father of all, who is above all, and through all, and in you all.

Ephesians 4:1-6 NKJV

¹² Just as a body, though one, has many parts, but all its many parts form one body, so it is with Christ. ¹³ For we were all baptized by one Spirit so as to form one body— whether Jews or Gentiles, slave or free—and we were all given the one Spirit to drink. ¹⁴ Even so the body is not made up of one part but of many.

¹⁵ Now if the foot should say, "Because I am not a hand, I do not belong to the body," it would not for that reason stop being part of the body. ¹⁶ And if the ear should say, "Because I am not an eye, I do not belong to the body," it would not for that reason stop being part of the body. ¹⁷ If the whole body were an eye, where would the sense of hearing be? If the whole body were an ear, where would the sense of smell be? ¹⁸ But in fact God has placed the parts in the body, every one of them, just as he wanted them to be. ¹⁹ If they were all one part, where would the body be? ²⁰ As it is, there are many parts, but one body.

²¹ The eye cannot say to the hand, "I don't need you!" And the head cannot say to the feet, "I don't need you!" ²² On the contrary, those parts of the body that seem to be weaker are indispensable, ²³ and the parts that we think are less honorable we treat with special honor. And the parts that are unpresentable are treated with special modesty, ²⁴ while our presentable parts need no special treatment. But God

*has put the body together, giving greater honor to the parts
that lacked it, ²⁵ so that there should be no division in the
body, but that its parts should have equal concern for each
other. ²⁶ If one part suffers, every part suffers with it; if one
part is honored, every part rejoices with it.
²⁷ Now you are the Body of Christ, and each one of you is a
part of it.*

1 Corinthians 12:12-27 NIV

In both of these passages, the Apostle Paul reveals to us that unity is something that all Christians should strive for, because it attracts honor to all parts of the Body of Christ. Moreover, at the beginning of the book of 1 Corinthians, Paul begins by expressing another very important aspect of unity as registered in 1 Corinthians 1:10-13 which says:

*¹⁰ Now I plead with you, brethren, by the name of our Lord
Jesus Christ, that you all speak the same thing, and that
there be no divisions among you, but that you be perfectly
joined together in the same mind and in the same judgment.
¹¹ For it has been declared to me concerning you, my
brethren, by those of Chloe's household, that there are
contentions among you. ¹² Now I say this, that each of you
says, "I am of Paul," or "I am of Apollos," or "I am of
Cephas," or "I am of Christ." ¹³ Is Christ divided? Was
Paul crucified for you? Or were you baptized in the name of
Paul?*

1 Corinthians 1:10-13 NKJV

Here, the Apostle Paul reveals to us that unity can protect us from giving each other the glory that only belongs to Jesus Christ. Now why was this so crucially important for him to point out? I believe, in addition to the unfortunate reality revealed in 1 Corinthians regarding the divisions that existed amongst the believers in Corinth, it was also because of what Paul learned from the Apostle John who registered the following favorable verses spoken by our Lord Jesus Christ in John 17:20-23 which says:

> *[20] I do not pray for these alone, but also for those who will believe in Me through their word; [21] that they all may be one, as You, Father, are in Me, and I in You; that they also may be one in Us, that the world may believe that You sent Me. [22] And the glory which You gave Me I have given them, that they may be one just as We are one: [23] I in them, and You in Me; that they may be made perfect in one, and that the world may know that You have sent Me, and have loved them as You have loved Me.*
>
> *John 17:20-23 NKJV*

In this scripture passage, Christ reveals to us that one of His greatest prayers during His passion week, just two days before He was crucified, was focused on unity. In fact, even after Christ's resurrection, in John 21:1-7, 15-17, He emphasizes just how paramount unity was in connection to the restoration of the Apostle Peter and Peter's future role in the Church which included the days leading up to Pentecost, the Day of Pentecost, and the days after Pentecost. Consider the following:

> *[1] After these things Jesus showed Himself again to the disciples at the Sea of Tiberias, and in this way He showed Himself: [2] Simon Peter, Thomas called the Twin, Nathanael of Cana in Galilee, the sons of Zebedee, and two others of His disciples were together. [3] Simon Peter said to them, "I am going fishing."*
> *They said to him, "We are going with you also." They went out and immediately got into the boat, and that night they caught nothing. [4] But when the morning had now come, Jesus stood on the shore; yet the disciples did not know that*

it was Jesus. ^{5} Then Jesus said to them, "Children, have you any food?"

They answered Him, "No."

^{6} And He said to them, "Cast the net on the right side of the boat, and you will find some." So they cast, and now they were not able to draw it in because of the multitude of fish.

^{7} Therefore that disciple whom Jesus loved said to Peter, "It is the Lord!" Now when Simon Peter heard that it was the Lord, he put on his outer garment (for he had removed it), and plunged into the sea.

^{15} So when they had eaten breakfast, Jesus said to Simon Peter, "Simon, son of Jonah, do you love Me more than these?"

He said to Him, "Yes, Lord; You know that I love You."

He said to him, "Feed My lambs."

^{16} He said to him again a second time, "Simon, son of Jonah, do you love Me?"

He said to Him, "Yes, Lord; You know that I love You."

He said to him, "Tend My sheep."

^{17} He said to him the third time, "Simon, son of Jonah, do you love Me?" Peter was grieved because He said to him the third time, "Do you love Me?"

And he said to Him, "Lord, You know all things; You know that I love You."

Jesus said to him, "Feed My sheep."

John 21:1-7; 15-17 NKJV

Through this scripture passage, Jesus Christ reveals to us the restoration of the Apostle Peter occurred within the context of unity also known as community. With community in mind, we should consider how unity was extremely essential for the primitive church as registered in Acts 2:41-47 which says:

[41] Then those who gladly received his word were baptized; and that day about three thousand souls were added to them. [42] And they continued steadfastly in the apostles' doctrine and fellowship, in the breaking of bread, and in prayers. [43] Then fear came upon every soul, and many wonders and signs were done through the apostles. [44] Now all who believed were together, and had all things in common, [45] and sold their possessions and goods, and divided them among all, as anyone had need.
[46] So continuing daily with one accord in the temple, and breaking bread from house to house, they ate their food with gladness and simplicity of heart, [47] praising God and having favor with all the people. And the Lord added to the Church daily those who were being saved.

Acts 2:41-47 NKJV

From this passage, we can concretely conclude that unity, like the rudiment of prayer, not only provokes revival, but also sustains and spreads revival beyond our lives to the lives of those around us. Moreover, there are plenty of other Bible passages that reveal and reiterate the same powerful truths about unity releasing revival. Yet with all that said, I have to admit all of this was not that obvious to me, although I had been born into a Pentecostal Christian family, was raised by my parents who became pastors when I was 2 years old, and I had been in church pastoral ministry ever since 1997.

Consequently, I needed to come to a full realization of the reverent relevance of unity, with regards to revival. With that said, allow me to share more of my personal testimony from the first few months of 2010. At that point in time, as I mentioned in the introduction of this book, I was coming out of an 18-month season of depression. Soon after, I went on a 40-day fast from the late evening of February 28th through April 9th. During that time, Pastor Matthew Hagee anointed me and prayed for me together with the younger pastoral leadership of Cornerstone Church on Tuesday, March 9th during one of our monthly

Joshua's Generation Prayer Meetings. Pastor Matthew anointed me with oil and specifically prayed for me to receive an anointing for unity, not revival, although he knew I had started a 40-day fast for revival nine days prior. Hence, I confess my initial human reaction to his prayer was not very favorable, since I wanted him to anoint me for revival and pray for that instead.

However, God quickly revealed to me the reason why He had Pastor Matthew anoint me and pray for me with regards to unity, was because unity was the one of five reverent rudiments for revival that I was grossly weak in having in my life and ministry. Additionally and soon after, God helped me to become acutely aware that unity was and still is one of the revival rudiments most severely lacking in the Body of Jesus Christ. Therefore, I needed to heed to what God was revealing to me to be one of the greatest needs in my life and in Christ's body. Once I accepted this revelation, then the Lord gave me a deeper revelation regarding why unity is so important to God and so imperative to His people, especially to His ministers.

In a time in which mental health is hugely important for all humanity especially for ministers, and in times in which many ministers are experiencing seasons of depression during the current dark times associated with the negative impact of the COVID-19 global pandemic and rising racial tensions, too many of us are like the Prophet Elijah, in a negative way. I say this because, although God gracefully utilizes our lives greatly, like He did with Elijah, to do great exploits in God's kingdom, after we experience spiritual high's, we then begin to experience spiritual low's. Subsequently, we begin to humanly feel we are all alone and quickly begin to think we are on our own. Furthermore, if we are not careful, we can then begin to believe we are the only one's God is utilizing greatly. Consequently, we can quickly find ourselves facing all sorts of spiritual, psychological, emotional, and physical exhaustion in our personal lives and ministry to the lives of others. In the end, like Elijah, we might even find ourselves seeking to prematurely end our time in kingdom ministry and even in human life. All of this can be observed in 1 Kings 18:36-46 and 1 Kings 19:1-18 which say:

[36] At the time of sacrifice, the prophet Elijah stepped forward and prayed: "LORD, the God of Abraham, Isaac and Israel, let it be known today that you are God in Israel and that I am your servant and have done all these things at your command. [37] Answer me, LORD, answer me, so these people will know that you, LORD, are God, and that you are turning their hearts back again."

[38] Then the fire of the LORD fell and burned up the sacrifice, the wood, the stones and the soil, and also licked up the water in the trench.

[39] When all the people saw this, they fell prostrate and cried, "The LORD—he is God! The LORD—he is God!"

[40] Then Elijah commanded them, "Seize the prophets of Baal. Don't let anyone get away!" They seized them, and Elijah had them brought down to the Kishon Valley and slaughtered there.

[41] And Elijah said to Ahab, "Go, eat and drink, for there is the sound of a heavy rain." [42] So Ahab went off to eat and drink, but Elijah climbed to the top of Carmel, bent down to the ground and put his face between his knees.

[43] "Go and look toward the sea," he told his servant. And he went up and looked.

"There is nothing there," he said.

Seven times Elijah said, "Go back."

[44] The seventh time the servant reported, "A cloud as small as a man's hand is rising from the sea."

So Elijah said, "Go and tell Ahab, 'Hitch up your chariot and go down before the rain stops you.'"

[45] Meanwhile, the sky grew black with clouds, the wind rose, a heavy rain started falling and Ahab rode off to Jezreel. [46] The power of the LORD came on Elijah and, tucking his cloak into his belt, he ran ahead of Ahab all the way to Jezreel.

1 Kings 18:36-46 NIV

[1] Now Ahab told Jezebel everything Elijah had done and how he had killed all the prophets with the sword. [2] So Jezebel sent a messenger to Elijah to say, "May the gods deal with me, be it ever so severely, if by this time tomorrow I do not make your life like that of one of them."

[3] Elijah was afraid and ran for his life. When he came to Beersheba in Judah, he left his servant there, [4] while he himself went a day's journey into the wilderness. He came to a broom bush, sat down under it and prayed that he might die. "I have had enough, LORD," he said. "Take my life; I am no better than my ancestors." [5] Then he lay down under the bush and fell asleep.

All at once an angel touched him and said, "Get up and eat." [6] He looked around, and there by his head was some bread baked over hot coals, and a jar of water. He ate and drank and then lay down again.

[7] The angel of the LORD came back a second time and touched him and said, "Get up and eat, for the journey is too much for you." [8] So he got up and ate and drank. Strengthened by that food, he traveled forty days and forty nights until he reached Horeb, the mountain of God. [9] There he went into a cave and spent the night.

And the word of the LORD came to him: "What are you doing here, Elijah?"

[10] He replied, "I have been very zealous for the LORD God Almighty. The Israelites have rejected your covenant, torn down your altars, and put your prophets to death with the sword. I am the only one left, and now they are trying to kill me too."

[11] The LORD said, "Go out and stand on the mountain in the presence of the LORD, for the LORD is about to pass by."

*Then a great and powerful wind tore the mountains apart
and shattered the rocks before the LORD, but the LORD was
not in the wind. After the wind there was an earthquake, but
the LORD was not in the earthquake. ^{12} After the earthquake
came a fire, but the LORD was not in the fire. And after the
fire came a gentle whisper. ^{13} When Elijah heard it, he
pulled his cloak over his face and went out and stood at the
mouth of the cave.*

*Then a voice said to him, "What are you doing here,
Elijah?"*

^{14} *He replied, "I have been very zealous for the LORD God
Almighty. The Israelites have rejected your covenant, torn
down your altars, and put your prophets to death with the
sword. I am the only one left, and now they are trying to kill
me too."*

^{15} *The LORD said to him, "Go back the way you came, and
go to the Desert of Damascus. When you get there, anoint
Hazael king over Aram. ^{16} Also, anoint Jehu son of Nimshi
king over Israel, and anoint Elisha son of Shaphat from
Abel Meholah to succeed you as prophet. ^{17} Jehu will put to
death any who escape the sword of Hazael, and Elisha will
put to death any who escape the sword of Jehu. ^{18} Yet I
reserve seven thousand in Israel—all whose knees have not
bowed down to Baal and whose mouths have not kissed
him."*

1 Kings 19:1-18 NIV

Therefore, it is worth noting that the Prophet Elijah convinced
himself that he was all alone instead of believing there were 7,000 others
like him, just as God had told Elijah. This isolation resulted in a
premature termination of his ministry on earth. Therefore, God nor we
can afford to have that happen again in our lifetime. We must unite with
the figurative "7,000 others" to be personally revived, so our personal
revival can then result in the corporate revival of our families,

congregations, communities, cities, states, nation, and beyond. In fact, I wholeheartedly believe that is what happened to and through the life of the Apostle Peter, as noted in Acts 1:12-14 and Acts 2:1-4 which say:

> *12 Then they returned to Jerusalem from the mount called Olivet, which is near Jerusalem, a Sabbath day's journey. 13 And when they had entered, they went up into the upper room where they were staying: Peter, James, John, and Andrew; Philip and Thomas; Bartholomew and Matthew; James the son of Alphaeus and Simon the Zealot; and Judas the son of James. 14 These all continued with one accord in prayer and supplication, with the women and Mary the mother of Jesus, and with His brothers.*
>
> *Acts 1:12-14 NKJV*

> *1 When the Day of Pentecost had fully come, they were all with one accord in one place. 2 And suddenly there came a sound from heaven, as of a rushing mighty wind, and it filled the whole house where they were sitting. 3 Then there appeared to them divided tongues, as of fire, and one sat upon each of them. 4 And they were all filled with the Holy Spirit and began to speak with other tongues, as the Spirit gave them utterance.*
>
> *Acts 2:1-4 NKJV*

Therefore, we must become like the Apostle Peter, who although he had miserably failed Jesus, he was miraculously restored by Jesus through the importance of unity in community. When I consider this, I am reminded of another part of my personal testimony and revival experience I touched on in the introduction of this book. Ten days after my first 40-day fast from February 28th through April 9th, God led me to go on a second 40-day fast, which strangely enough had nothing to do with fasting food, but did have everything to do with fasting sleep. After unsuccessfully negotiating with God in letting Him know I would accept

His invitation as long as I could continue to pray specifically for revival, He compassionately and concisely convicted me. He made it clear that I was to solely pray for unity instead, from 11:00 p.m. to 1:00 a.m. from April 19th through May 28th.

When I asked Him why He was asking me to pray during that specific time period, He led me to understand those two hours represented the omega and alpha hours of a 24-hour period. Correspondingly and biblically speaking, since God is the Alpha and Omega, Beginning and End, First and Last, He wanted me to give Him those two hours in prayer as a type of fast, with regards to not sleeping. Therefore, I somewhat reluctantly agreed, but He graciously and mercifully dealt with me. Then I experienced a unity encounter and epiphany around the 25th day of this second 40-day fast. Although I had missed my prayer time that night, due to oversleeping on my evening nap before normally waking up at 10:30-45 p.m. to begin praying at 11:00 p.m., I instead woke up at 1:30 a.m. Consequently, I sensed a major weight of condemnation come over me.

However, the Lord quickly reminded me there is no condemnation in Christ Jesus according to Romans 8:1, and He told me to shake it off and go spend time with Him. So I did just that. However, little did I know what would ensue moments later would be the Lord ushering me into His presence for the following five hours of prayer and scripture reading specifically focused on the subject, emphasis, and importance of unity. In fact, the culminating scripture passage He led me to was John 17:1-23. Before I knew it, all I could pray for was for the Lord to unite His church, His people, His ministers and leaders, especially those ministering to youth and young adults as I was doing so at the time.

The next night, God graced me to get back on track with praying each night from 11:00 p.m. to 1:00 a.m., and by His grace and with His strength, I did so for the following fifteen days until the end of the 40-day prayer fast which ended on May 28th. During that time, God graced me with continued revelation about being less like the Old Testament Elijah and being more like the New Testament Peter, regardless of

Peter's major mistakes as noted in Matthew 16, Luke 22, and John 21. To better understand what the Lord showed me, let us consider the following passages of scripture:

> [13] *When Jesus came into the region of Caesarea Philippi, He asked His disciples, saying, "Who do men say that I, the Son of Man, am?"*
>
> [14] *So they said, "Some say John the Baptist, some Elijah, and others Jeremiah or one of the prophets."*
>
> [15] *He said to them, "But who do you say that I am?"*
>
> [16] *Simon Peter answered and said, "You are the Christ, the Son of the living God."*
>
> [17] *Jesus answered and said to him, "Blessed are you, Simon Bar-Jonah, for flesh and blood has not revealed this to you, but My Father who is in heaven.* [18] *And I also say to you that you are Peter, and on this rock I will build My church, and the gates of Hades shall not prevail against it.* [19] *And I will give you the keys of the kingdom of heaven, and whatever you bind on earth will be bound in heaven, and whatever you loose on earth will be loosed in heaven."*
>
> [20] *Then He commanded His disciples that they should tell no one that He was Jesus the Christ.*
>
> [21] *From that time Jesus began to show to His disciples that He must go to Jerusalem, and suffer many things from the elders and chief priests and scribes, and be killed, and be raised the third day.*
>
> [22] *Then Peter took Him aside and began to rebuke Him, saying, "Far be it from You, Lord; this shall not happen to You!"*
>
> [23] *But He turned and said to Peter, "Get behind Me, Satan! You are an offense to Me, for you are not mindful of the things of God, but the things of men."*
>
> *Matthew 16:13-23 NKJV*

28 But you are those who have continued with Me in My trials. 29 And I bestow upon you a kingdom, just as My Father bestowed one upon Me, 30 that you may eat and drink at My table in My kingdom, and sit on thrones judging the twelve tribes of Israel."

31 And the Lord said, "Simon, Simon! Indeed, Satan has asked for you, that he may sift you as wheat. 32 But I have prayed for you, that your faith should not fail; and when you have returned to Me, strengthen your brethren."

33 But he said to Him, "Lord, I am ready to go with You, both to prison and to death."

34 Then He said, "I tell you, Peter, the rooster shall not crow this day before you will deny three times that you know Me."

54 Having arrested Him, they led Him and brought Him into the high priest's house. But Peter followed at a distance. 55 Now when they had kindled a fire in the midst of the courtyard and sat down together, Peter sat among them. 56 And a certain servant girl, seeing him as he sat by the fire, looked intently at him and said, "This man was also with Him."

57 But he denied Him, saying, "Woman, I do not know Him."

58 And after a little while another saw him and said, "You also are of them."

But Peter said, "Man, I am not!"

59 Then after about an hour had passed, another confidently affirmed, saying, "Surely this fellow also was with Him, for he is a Galilean."

60 But Peter said, "Man, I do not know what you are saying!"

Immediately, while he was still speaking, the rooster crowed. 61 And the Lord turned and looked at Peter. Then

Peter remembered the word of the Lord, how He had said to him, "Before the rooster crows, you will deny Me three times." [62] So Peter went out and wept bitterly.

Luke 22:28-34; 54-62 NKJV

From these passages of scripture, intriguingly and interestingly enough, we see that in Matthew 16, Peter received his calling, and yet he failed, while in Luke 22, Peter received a promotion, and yet he failed again. Additionally, when we consider John 21, which we already looked at earlier in this chapter, we can observe that Peter, who had failed miserably on multiple occasions, is then restored miraculously in the context of unity in community with six other disciples.

Yet, before Peter was miraculously restored, I believe he might have had a premeditated plan to fail even more miserably than he did so in denying Jesus Christ. Allow me to explain. In John 21, when Peter told the other six disciples he was with at the time, that he was going to go fishing, and he did not invite them, could it be that he was considering taking his life in a similar way that Judas did? I say this based on what Jesus said in Matthew 18:6, Mark 9:42, and Luke 17:1-2 which say:

[6] But whoever causes one of these little ones who believe in Me to sin, it would be better for him if a millstone were hung around his neck, and he were drowned in the depth of the sea.

Matthew 18:6 NKJV

[42] But whoever causes one of these little ones who believe in Me to stumble, it would be better for him if a millstone were hung around his neck, and he were thrown into the sea.

Mark 9:42 NKJV

[1] Then He said to the disciples, "It is impossible that no offenses should come, but woe to him through whom they do come! [2] It would be better for him if a millstone were hung

around his neck, and he were thrown into the sea, than that he should offend one of these little ones. "

Luke 17:1-2 NKJV

Intriguingly enough, all three of these passages, reveal to us the severity of causing others to stumble, sin against, and offend the little ones in life and in the faith. While this certainly does refer to doing so against actual children, I believe it can also refer to doing so against those who are young in the faith, such as Peter's peer disciples. Correspondingly, in addition to what Judas had done in betraying Jesus Christ while not living in unity with the other disciples and subsequently taking his own life, could it be that Peter perhaps planned to do something similar? Could it be that when Peter said in John 21:3 to the other six disciples he was going fishing, that he was actually planning on taking his own life too by tying a millstone around his neck and casting himself into the sea? Considering that Peter had denied Jesus Christ three times while influencing the other ten disciples to abandon Jesus, it seems very likely Peter may have been considering such a grave act.

However, could it also be that what kept Peter from following through with the act of taking his own life was the fact that he had true friends who were there for him? Could it be that it was the authentic friendships Peter had with the other disciples that kept him from taking his own life? Could it be that it was unity in the context of community that contributed greatly to the revival of Peter which then in turn led to the revival of other disciples and believers like Peter? I wholeheartedly believe this could have very well been the case, because, in my own personal experience, when I battled depression, although I did not struggle with thoughts of suicide, I did pray several times for the Lord to let me go to sleep one night and wake up in His presence only by His grace and through His mercy.

However, one of the few things that helped me combat those woeful thoughts, feelings, and desires to quit on life and ministry altogether, was the unity in community I personally experienced within the context of my family, the pastoral staff of Cornerstone Church, and fellow ministers in the family and kingdom of God. In fact, I truly believe this happened because there is revival power in unity, as noted in Matthew 18:18-20 which says:

> [18] *Assuredly, I say to you, whatever you bind on earth will be bound in heaven, and whatever you loose on earth will be loosed in heaven.*
> [19] *Again I say to you that if two of you agree on earth concerning anything that they ask, it will be done for them by My Father in heaven.* [20] *For where two or three are gathered together in My name, I am there in the midst of them.*
>
> *Matthew 18:18-20 NKJV*

Now in contrast, let us consider Judas who did not experience the context of unity in community, as noted in Matthew 27:1-5 and Acts 1:15-20 which say:

> [1] *When morning came, all the chief priests and elders of the people plotted against Jesus to put Him to death.* [2] *And when they had bound Him, they led Him away and delivered Him to Pontius Pilate the governor.*
> [3] *Then Judas, His betrayer, seeing that He had been condemned, was remorseful and brought back the thirty pieces of silver to the chief priests and elders,* [4] *saying, "I have sinned by betraying innocent blood."*
> *And they said, "What is that to us? You see to it!"*
> [5] *Then he threw down the pieces of silver in the temple and departed, and went and hanged himself.*
>
> *Matthew 27:1-5 NKJV*

> [15] *And in those days Peter stood up in the midst of the disciples (altogether the number of names was about a hundred and twenty), and said,* [16] *"Men and brethren, this*

Scripture had to be fulfilled, which the Holy Spirit spoke
before by the mouth of David concerning Judas, who
became a guide to those who arrested Jesus; [17] *for he was*
numbered with us and obtained a part in this ministry."
[18] *(Now this man purchased a field with the wages of*
iniquity; and falling headlong, he burst open in the middle
and all his entrails gushed out. [19] *And it became known to*
all those dwelling in Jerusalem; so that field is called in
their own language, Akel Dama, that is, Field of Blood.)
[20] *"For it is written in the Book of Psalms:*
'Let his dwelling place be desolate,
And let no one live in it';
and,
'Let another take his office.'"

Acts 1:15-20 NKJV

In these passages of scripture, we see Judas did not live in the
context of unity in community with the other disciples. In fact, he
isolated himself from the disciples and betrayed Jesus Christ to the chief
priests and elders of the Jewish people at the time. Consequently, when
Judas realized the gravity of the wrong he had done against Jesus Christ,
he went back to the chief priests and elders to let them know of his
wrong, and they rejected him. At that moment of isolation and rejection,
which is the complete opposite of unity in community, Judas resorted to
hanging himself, instead of being restored and revived like Peter would
soon after experience.

On the other hand, Peter, who had miserably failed Jesus Christ,
and was shortly afterwards miraculously restored by Christ within the
context of unity, thereafter, led the other disciples to be restored through
the same kind of unity, as especially noted in Acts 2:14-16 which says:

[14] *But Peter, standing up with the eleven, raised his voice*
and said to them, "Men of Judea and all who dwell in
Jerusalem, let this be known to you, and heed my words.

199

[15] For these are not drunk, as you suppose, since it is only the third hour of the day. [16] But this is what was spoken by the Prophet Joel:

Acts 2:14-16 NKJV

Through this passage and those we have previously considered in this chapter, together with the testimony of Peter's life and ministry, we see how unity was an essential reverent rudiment for revival which occurred in his life and in the lives of his friends, the 120 disciples, the 3,000 converts on the Day of Pentecost, and beyond.

When I consider this, it reminds me of an additional part of my personal testimony I referenced in the introduction of this book. After the second 40-day fast, during which God had me focus on praying for unity, the Revival NOW Conference, led by Eileen Vincent and Natalie Hardy of City Reachers of San Antonio, Texas, occurred on the weekend of June 11-13th. In addition to having great ministers of the Lord such as Chuck Pierce, Hector Torres, and Johnny Ortiz minister at this conference, Eileen and Natalie sensed from the Lord to grace me with the opportunity to also minister. Therefore, on Saturday night, June 12th, over 600 Hispanic, Black, and White youth and young adults gathered together from at least twenty denominational and non-denominational youth and young adult ministries from all over San Antonio and beyond. It was in that service I shared a very condensed version of this "Revival Now" message. By the time we reached the moment for the altar call, hundreds of young people of multiple ethnicities, ministries, and denominations had given and rededicated their lives to Jesus Christ and began to cry out to God for revival now. It was a surreal and supernatural powerful moment in God's time for all of our lives.

Then the following month and the months thereafter, City Reachers and a group of us, multiethnic youth and young adult pastors, throughout San Antonio began having monthly nights of worship and intercession with various non-denominational and denominational ministries from all over the region. Shortly after initiating this unified worship and intercession initiative for more revival, God impressed upon

200

my heart to establish a multiethnic interdenominational relational fellowship for youth and young adult pastors and leaders in San Antonio. After sharing this with Pastor Matthew Hagee, he gracefully gave me his blessing to launch it together with twelve very influential Hispanic, Black, and White American youth and adult pastors from the city: 1. Johnny Ortiz, 2. Michael Fernandez, 3. Michael Hernandez, 4. Jarrell Flowers, 5. David Robinson, 6. Matthew Bell, 7. Gavin Rogers, 8. Oscar Guajardo, 9. Sammy Lopez, 10. David Mayorga, 11. David Martin, and 12. Tina Hidy-Marlin. It is worth mentioning these great ministers were from great non-denominational churches and denominations such as the Assemblies of God, Church of God, San Antonio Baptist Association, United Methodist Church, Seventh Day Adventist, and the Catholic Church.

As for the multiethnic interdenominational relational fellowship itself, we called it "UNITE." Its name was primarily based on Pastor Matthew's anointing and prayer over my life for unity and the unity prayer focus the Lord gave me during the second 40-day fast He led me on highlighted by His prayer for unity in John 17. Eventually, we launched "UNITE" in January of 2011 at TriPoint – A Center for Life facility, with our first monthly lunch meeting being attended by approximately 90 multiethnic youth, young adult, and adult pastors and leaders from over 50 non-denominational and denominational churches in San Antonio. God gracefully and mercifully used "UNITE" to usher in the beginning of a revival amongst young people throughout the city of San Antonio. In two years' time, from 2011 to 2013, over 50 ministries throughout the city joined together with "UNITE," and approximately 300 leaders in our city attended at least one or more of our unity and revival events for youth and young adult pastors, student leaders, and young people in our city. It was during these gatherings where a combined total of thousands of multiethnic youth and young adults were powerfully revived by our Lord, as we continued to unite in prayer, worship, periodic fasting, and the receiving of God's word.

Included in those events, we united with regional and national ministries and movements such as the local Trinity Broadcast Network in

San Antonio, Fellowship of Christian Athletes, and God Belongs In My City led by my dear friend, Pastor Daniel Sanabria, of Brooklyn, New York. It is worth mentioning that "UNITE" continues to this very day in 2020, and is now led by my friend, Pastor Joel Garza, who I was graced to add to our "UNITE" core team in 2013 before I transitioned out of my role as its lead facilitator. Now, Pastor Joel and his current "UNITE" core team continue to gather multiethnic youth, young adults, and adult pastors and leaders from non-denominational and denominational ministries for the same purpose of ushering in the next great awakening into San Antonio and its surrounding areas.

Back to 2011, in April of that year, Pastor Matthew then graced me with the opportunity to serve as the Cornerstone College and Career Young Adult Pastor, in addition to continuing to serve as the High School Youth Pastor. Together with my great staff, we hosted monthly city-wide youth and young adult rallies for multiethnic young people throughout our city and beyond. At these rallies, we were blessed to have guest ministers such as Lou Engle, Eddie James, Jeremy Johnson, Tim Ross, Robert Madu, Matthew Bismark, Josh Radford, Joe Oden, Frank Hechavarria, Gabby Mejia, Mark Vega, Kari Jobe, Rick Pino, Jake Hamilton, and others come minister and help us keep the flames of revival growing. Then in January of 2013, Mildred and I, together with our dear friends Pastors Michael and Lucy Fernandez, Pastors Johnny and Ruth Ortiz, and Pastors Josue and Benita Holguin, legally established and officially launched our evangelistic ministry, "De Jesus Ministries." Since 2013 we have ministered to over 150,000 people of all ages in the U.S., Puerto Rico, Mexico, and Costa Rica, in addition to many more thousands of people by way of social media, YouTube, and appearances on local TBN channels in San Antonio and Houston and the national TBN Salsa program in Dallas, Texas.

I share all of this, first, to give God the glory for all He did to us and through us because of the unity He graced us with which is a great testament to the rudiment of unity in Christ for revival. Secondly, I share this, only by His grace, to emphatically express how extremely important unity is for revival, especially within the context of the current great and grave need our nation has for racial reconciliation. With that in mind, I believe it would be helpful to share with you that some of the greatest unity principles and proclamations the Lord taught me during that revival season was the following fivefold statement of unity in Christ's kingdom:

1. We are in Christ's kingdom to complete, not to compete.
2. We are in Christ's kingdom to complement, not to contradict.
3. We are in Christ's kingdom to fulfill, not to frustrate.
4. We are in Christ's kingdom to be inclusive, not to be exclusive.
5. We are in Christ's kingdom to be united by His Spirit within, not to be divided by the color of our skin.

In fact, the Lord revealed to me that our individual leadership and ministries are each like individual puzzle pieces which when left alone, can be a bit puzzling. Yet, when we, as His puzzle pieces, unite in Christ, then we can form a masterpiece. However, it is not just any masterpiece, because it is the Master's piece, and that piece is complete in Christ. Why? Our Lord Jesus Christ and His kingdom is all about unity.

Even more recently, Mildred and I joined Lou Engle Ministries in fasting this 2020 year from March 1st through April 9th. As a result, Mildred and I sensed from the Lord to take Holy Communion almost every day from March 1st through April 9th and even beyond. Correspondingly, God has revealed to us through His word and the Holy Spirit's teaching that a major part of what the Lord's Supper, also known as Holy Communion, is all about is unity. Furthermore, the actual word "communion" has the word union in it.

Additionally, when we recently considered 1 Corinthians 11 more comprehensively from the vantage point of unity, we discovered that taking the Holy Communion in an unworthy manner is not only about having unconfessed sin in our lives. In addition to that scriptural reality, it is also specifically about the real disunity that has been allowed within the Body of Christ we are all supposed to be a unified part of. In

203

other words, if we are not united with our multiethnic brothers and sisters in Christ, and we take the Lord's Supper, then we are actually taking it in an unworthy manner. This is a grave sin, since the Lord Jesus Christ gave up His life so we all could be one with Him and with each other through Him. To help us understand this, let us consider 1 Corinthians 11:17-34 which says:

> [17] *In the following directives I have no praise for you, for your meetings do more harm than good.* [18] *In the first place, I hear that when you come together as a church, there are divisions among you, and to some extent I believe it.* [19] *No doubt there have to be differences among you to show which of you have God's approval.* [20] *So then, when you come together, it is not the Lord's Supper you eat,* [21] *for when you are eating, some of you go ahead with your own private suppers. As a result, one person remains hungry and another gets drunk.* [22] *Don't you have homes to eat and drink in? Or do you despise the Church of God by humiliating those who have nothing? What shall I say to you? Shall I praise you? Certainly not in this matter!* [23] *For I received from the Lord what I also passed on to you: The Lord Jesus, on the night he was betrayed, took bread,* [24] *and when he had given thanks, he broke it and said, "This is my body, which is for you; do this in remembrance of me."* [25] *In the same way, after supper he took the cup, saying, "This cup is the new covenant in my blood; do this, whenever you drink it, in remembrance of me."* [26] *For whenever you eat this bread and drink this cup, you proclaim the Lord's death until he comes.* [27] *So then, whoever eats the bread or drinks the cup of the Lord in an unworthy manner will be guilty of sinning against the body and blood of the Lord.* [28] *Everyone ought to examine themselves before they eat of the bread and drink from the cup.* [29] *For those who eat and drink without*

discerning the Body of Christ eat and drink judgment on themselves. [30] That is why many among you are weak and sick, and a number of you have fallen asleep. [31] But if we were more discerning with regard to ourselves, we would not come under such judgment. [32] Nevertheless, when we are judged in this way by the Lord, we are being disciplined so that we will not be finally condemned with the world. [33] So then, my brothers and sisters, when you gather to eat, you should all eat together. [34] Anyone who is hungry should eat something at home, so that when you meet together it may not result in judgment.
And when I come I will give further directions.

1 Corinthians 11:17-34 NIV

From this passage, we can be reminded that when we receive Holy Communion, we are remembering our Lord Jesus Christ's death, which mainly occurred to reconcile or unite lost humanity to His Heavenly Father and to reconcile or unite fragmented humanity to each other through Jesus Christ. This is further evident in 2 Corinthians 5:18-21 which says:

[18] Now all things are of God, who has reconciled us to Himself through Jesus Christ, and has given us the ministry of reconciliation, [19] that is, that God was in Christ reconciling the world to Himself, not imputing their trespasses to them, and has committed to us the word of reconciliation.
[20] Now then, we are ambassadors for Christ, as though God were pleading through us: we implore you on Christ's behalf, be reconciled to God. [21] For He made Him who knew no sin to be sin for us, that we might become the righteousness of God in Him.

2 Corinthians 5:18-21 NKJV

Correspondingly, during the current crucial times in which racial tensions across our nation continue to rise to all-time highs and individual persons, groups, and organizations seek to be in the limelight, I believe God desires to remind us that what He is doing in these last days is not about exalting any particular man, woman, minister, ministry or movement of God. Additionally, He is reminding us that what He is doing in these end-times is not about any specific ethnic group in our nation and beyond. However, instead, what God is doing is all about, and will always be about, exalting the One Messiah sent from God to all humanity in desperate need of Him, because in His time, God will rapture His multiethnic church from all over the globe to be united with Christ in the heavens above, as noted in Revelation 5:5-10 and Revelation 7:9-10 which say:

> [5] *Then one of the elders said to me, "Do not weep! See, the Lion of the tribe of Judah, the Root of David, has triumphed. He is able to open the scroll and its seven seals."*
> [6] *Then I saw a Lamb, looking as if it had been slain, standing at the center of the throne, encircled by the four living creatures and the elders. The Lamb had seven horns and seven eyes, which are the seven spirits of God sent out into all the earth.* [7] *He went and took the scroll from the right hand of him who sat on the throne.* [8] *And when he had taken it, the four living creatures and the twenty-four elders fell down before the Lamb. Each one had a harp and they were holding golden bowls full of incense, which are the prayers of God's people.* [9] *And they sang a new song, saying:*
> *"You are worthy to take the scroll*
>   *and to open its seals,*
> *because you were slain,*
>   *and with your blood you purchased for God*
>   *persons from every tribe and language and people and*

nation.

[10] You have made them to be a kingdom and priests to serve our God,

   and they will reign on the earth."

Revelation 5:6-10 NIV

[9] After this I looked, and there before me was a great multitude that no one could count, from every nation, tribe, people and language, standing before the throne and before the Lamb. They were wearing white robes and were holding palm branches in their hands. [10] And they cried out in a loud voice:

"Salvation belongs to our God,
who sits on the throne,
and to the Lamb."

Revelation 7:9-10 NIV

Therefore, now more than ever, I believe the multicolored, multilingual, and multicultural Body of Jesus Christ must unite with Christ and with each other in Christ, regardless of age, gender, ethnicity, nationality, profession, social class, and any other human classification. We are one in Christ, through His precious blood, and by His Holy Spirit, and it is time we see God's kingdom come and His will be done on earth as it is in Heaven. Now, if you believe this with me, I invite you to read the next and final chapter of this book which has been written with the end-goal of recruiting and releasing you to join me and countless of others in becoming revivalists. History is in the making for the next great awakening, and our unity in and with Jesus Christ will prepare, position, and posture us to receive revival now!

CHAPTER 12
IT'S TIME TO RECRUIT REVIVALISTS NOW!

Congratulations on finally arriving to the final chapter of this book. I commend each of you on your determination to read this written work in its entirety. Please know, that in this 2020 year and during this new decade, I believe you are a vital part of a revival remnant God is now raising up in every single sector of our society including those of government, military, education, business, medicine, athletics, entertainment, music, and more. Consequently, if by any chance you have not read all of this book yet, I highly encourage you to do so, before you proceed with this book's last portion. I say this because I wholeheartedly believe there is a scriptural and spiritual sequence to this written work that, in its purposeful order, best prepares you for what you will read in this final chapter and hopefully do in response to its call. In fact, the reason I say this is because the goal of this book is to lead us beyond reading it to being recruited by it.

In other words, I believe it is time for us to unite with our Lord Jesus Christ in recruiting revivalists now, because the time has arrived for us to go from personal revival to corporate revival, and from local revival to global revival. Correspondingly, I am deeply convinced God desires to release the kind of revival that can start with your house and my house and continue onto every schoolhouse, courthouse, jailhouse, and even the White House of our nation. Consequently, I believe revival in America could spread throughout all of the Americas and continue onto the rest of the world. Why? Because the whole world is in desperate need of revival now from our Lord Jesus Christ, and therefore needs you and me as His revivalists now.

Therefore, in preparing for all of that to happen, it would benefit us to recall Ephesians 5:14, which is interestingly enough first directed to an individual person, before it is directed to a group of people. Let us consider this very powerful verse which says:

> *[14] Therefore He says:*
> *"Awake, you who sleep,*
> *Arise from the dead,*
> *And Christ will give you light."*
>
> *Ephesians 5:14 NKJV*

When I consider this verse, I recall a life-lesson I have learned from God's word and through my own personal experience. The lesson is, that the majority of the time, if not all the time, revival has to first happen to you, before it can happen through you. What is so powerful about this, is that when each of us personally pursues the Lord for revival, then the revival we individually receive will have the potential to result in a corporate revival for many more people to receive as well. In fact, I believe it will be much more than we could ever imagine. This biblical revival truth is specifically registered in John 4:39-42 and John 12:9-11 which say:

> *[39] And many of the Samaritans of that city believed in Him because of the word of the woman who testified, "He told me all that I ever did." [40] So when the Samaritans had come*

210

to Him, they urged Him to stay with them; and He stayed there two days. ⁴¹ *And many more believed because of His own word.*
⁴² *Then they said to the woman, "Now we believe, not because of what you said, for we ourselves have heard Him and we know that this is indeed the Christ, the Savior of the world."*

John 4:39-42 NKJV

⁹ *Now a great many of the Jews knew that He was there; and they came, not for Jesus' sake only, but that they might also see Lazarus, whom He had raised from the dead.* ¹⁰ *But the chief priests plotted to put Lazarus to death also,*
¹¹ *because on account of him many of the Jews went away and believed in Jesus.*

John 12:9-11 NKJV

Intriguingly enough, in these two passages of scripture, we see that a personal revival happened first to a particular individual before it happened to a group of people. Specifically speaking, revival first occurred in the life of the Samaritan woman at the well, before revival occurred through her testimony to everyone in her city. Additionally, we see personal revival first took place in the life of Lazarus in his tomb, before it happened through his life to everyone in his living room and throughout his region. This is such a powerful truth, and I am sure it will soon apply to you, if it has not done so already.

For me, revival started in my personal life, but then moved onto my wife, our children, our families, youth and young adult ministries, our city, and beyond. In fact, by God's grace and for His glory, His revival work has moved to and through my life to over 150,000 lives all over the United States, Puerto Rico, and parts of Central America. Now through this book, only God knows what He will continue to do through His revival work in and through my life to many more hundreds of thousands in my nation and around the world.

Yet, what about you? What will God soon do to you and through you to so many around you? Just begin to imagine the greater revival God is going to bring to and through you to the multitudes. Although His revival work in you will start in your life, home, neighborhood, and community, God is able to also bring forth revival through your life to your city, state, nation, and beyond. Yes, He is able, and I am believing with you that what the Lord is going to do to you and through you is going to be huge. In fact, I believe your personal revival will contribute greatly to a collective corporate revival for a great multitude of believers.

Now to what extent can we expect corporate revival, when we let revival personally begin with us? The answer can be discovered when we consider the Prophet Ezekiel, the people of Israel, and their promised land as spoken of in Ezekiel 37:1-10 which says:

> [1] *The hand of the LORD was on me, and he brought me out by the Spirit of the LORD and set me in the middle of a valley; it was full of bones.* [2] *He led me back and forth among them, and I saw a great many bones on the floor of the valley, bones that were very dry.* [3] *He asked me, "Son of man, can these bones live?"*
> *I said, "Sovereign LORD, you alone know."*
> [4] *Then he said to me, "Prophesy to these bones and say to them, 'Dry bones, hear the word of the LORD!* [5] *This is what the Sovereign LORD says to these bones: I will make breath enter you, and you will come to life.* [6] *I will attach tendons to you and make flesh come upon you and cover you with skin; I will put breath in you, and you will come to life. Then you will know that I am the LORD.'"*
> [7] *So I prophesied as I was commanded. And as I was prophesying, there was a noise, a rattling sound, and the bones came together, bone to bone.* [8] *I looked, and tendons and flesh appeared on them and skin covered them, but there was no breath in them.*

⁹ Then he said to me, "Prophesy to the breath; prophesy,
son of man, and say to it, 'This is what the Sovereign LORD
says: Come, breath, from the four winds and breathe into
these slain, that they may live.'" ¹⁰ So I prophesied as he
commanded me, and breath entered them; they came to life
and stood up on their feet—a vast army.

Ezekiel 37:1-10 NIV

In this passage of scripture, we see that God first gives the Prophet Ezekiel a personal encounter or revival, if you will. Then, the move of God in Ezekiel's life leads to a corporate revival for the people of Israel. Correspondingly, Ezekiel and the people of Israel, who are revived and raised up as a vast army, are then prophetically informed by God through Ezekiel that they would be able to return to their land and once again possess the land God had promised to them and their descendants. What is so powerful about this is that this has literally happened in the past for the people of Israel and is continuing to happen in our present times with the nation and land of Israel.

Therefore, since I fully understand this, I also understand, that, in biblical and kingdom principle, it can additionally apply to us Christians who are revived and raised up in Jesus Christ through the power of His Holy Spirit so we can return to or possess once again what God has promised to His church in our nation and throughout the nations of the world. In other words, our personal revival in Christ, through the work of His Spirit, according to our Father's will, has the potential to result in a corporate revival of His church so we can possess what He has promised to us. This could include our homes, neighborhoods, communities, cities, states, nation, and so much more. In fact, I believe this prophetically and apostolically speaks to a coming local revival that will become a global revival.

Another example of this can be observed when we consider the Apostle Peter, the primitive church, and its sphere of influence, according to Acts 2:38-41, Acts 4:4, and Acts 17:5-6 which say:

[38] Then Peter said to them, "Repent, and let every one of you be baptized in the name of Jesus Christ for the remission of sins; and you shall receive the gift of the Holy Spirit. [39] For the promise is to you and to your children, and to all who are afar off, as many as the Lord our God will call."
[40] And with many other words he testified and exhorted them, saying, "Be saved from this perverse generation."
[41] Then those who gladly received his word were baptized; and that day about three thousand souls were added to them.

Acts 2:38-41 NKJV

[4] However, many of those who heard the word believed; and the number of the men came to be about five thousand.

Acts 4:4 NKJV

[5] But the Jews who were not persuaded, becoming envious, took some of the evil men from the marketplace, and gathering a mob, set all the city in an uproar and attacked the house of Jason, and sought to bring them out to the people. [6] But when they did not find them, they dragged Jason and some brethren to the rulers of the city, crying out, "These who have turned the world upside down have come here too."

Acts 17:5-6 NKJV

Similar in principle to what happened in Ezekiel 37, in Acts 2, 4, and 17, God utilized Peter's personal revival to result in the people's corporate revival which started in one city and continued eventually throughout the world. Correspondingly, Peter and the believers in the book of Acts were revived and raised up in Christ through the power of the Holy Spirit so they could possess or influence their land according to God's promise. The revival released a Godkind of a kingdom revolution.

The end result, in both instances of the Prophet Ezekiel and the Apostle Peter, was a divine moment in time that arrived for history to be made through a great awakening within God's people.

Now as I fast forward from Ezekiel and Peter to you and me in 2020 and the new decade we are presently in, I wholeheartedly believe we have arrived to another one of God's divine moments in history for humanity. Therefore, in our current time, it is extraordinarily imperative that we redeem the time, as stated in Ephesians 5:15-17 which says:

> [15] *See then that you walk circumspectly, not as fools but as wise,* [16] *redeeming the time, because the days are evil.* [17] *Therefore do not be unwise, but understand what the will of the Lord is.*
>
> *Ephesians 5:15-17 NKJV*

In redeeming the time in our present time, I believe God is calling us to: 1) be carefully watchful, 2) be spiritually wise, 3) realize the present evil times, 4) understand God's will for us, and 5) respond accordingly to His call to us for revival, because history is in the making for the next great awakening, and it is time for revival now. Yet, the question is, "Will you be a part of it, or apart from it?" "Will you respond to the call for revival now, or will you postpone the call for revival later?" I believe, pray, hope, and expect for you to say "yes" to God's call on your life for revival now.

Therefore, based on everything I have scripturally, spiritually, ministerially, and personally shared with you in this entire book, I invite you to accept the "40-Day Revival Now Challenge" I first accepted ten years ago in 2010 and then accepted again in this 2020 year. What exactly is that challenge? Here it is. In 2020 and over the course of this new decade, as God calls you to do so, give Him 40 days with a 20/20 vision focus on:

1. PRAYER
2. FASTING

3.   WORSHIP
4.   LIVING ACCORDING TO GOD'S WORD
5.   UNITY

Additionally, during your "40-Day Revival Now Challenge," I also encourage you to take Holy Communion and anoint yourself with anointing oil, as often as you sense the Lord leading you to do so. I humbly make this recommendation to you, due to my personal experience of doing so, together with Mildred, during this year and experiencing a greater measure of revival connected to it. After all, Holy Communion has everything to do with remembering what Jesus Christ did for us at the cross, and the anointing oil has everything to do with receiving what the Holy Spirit did for His church in the upper room.

Now in wrapping up this book, I invite you to begin your revival now journey by first asking our Lord Jesus Christ to baptize or re-baptize you with His Holy Spirit and fire as He did to the Apostle Peter and the 120 disciples on the Day of Pentecost according to Acts 2. This empowering Spirit baptism is based on Luke 3 and 12, and Acts 1, 9, 10, and 19, from which we should remember the corresponding following passages of scripture:

> [1] *When the Day of Pentecost had fully come, they were all with one accord in one place.* [2] *And suddenly there came a sound from heaven, as of a rushing mighty wind, and it filled the whole house where they were sitting.* [3] *Then there appeared to them divided tongues, as of fire, and one sat upon each of them.* [4] *And they were all filled with the Holy Spirit and began to speak with other tongues, as the Spirit gave them utterance.*
>
> *Acts 2:1-4 NKJV*

> [16] *John answered, saying to all, "I indeed baptize you with water; but One mightier than I is coming, whose sandal*

216

strap I am not worthy to loose. He will baptize you with the Holy Spirit and fire."

Luke 3:16 NKJV

⁴⁹ I came to send fire on the earth, and how I wish it were already kindled!

Luke 12:49 NKJV

⁴ And being assembled together with them, He commanded them not to depart from Jerusalem, but to wait for the Promise of the Father, "which," He said, "you have heard from Me; ⁵ for John truly baptized with water, but you shall be baptized with the Holy Spirit not many days from now."

Acts 1:4-5 NKJV

¹⁷ And Ananias went his way and entered the house; and laying his hands on him he said, "Brother Saul, the Lord Jesus, who appeared to you on the road as you came, has sent me that you may receive your sight and be filled with the Holy Spirit." ¹⁸ Immediately there fell from his eyes something like scales, and he received his sight at once; and he arose and was baptized.

Acts 9:17-18 NKJV

⁴⁴ While Peter was still speaking these words, the Holy Spirit fell upon all those who heard the word. ⁴⁵ And those of the circumcision who believed were astonished, as many as came with Peter, because the gift of the Holy Spirit had been poured out on the Gentiles also.

Acts 10:44-45 NKJV

¹ And it happened, while Apollos was at Corinth, that Paul, having passed through the upper regions, came to Ephesus.

217

And finding some disciples [2] he said to them, "Did you
receive the Holy Spirit when you believed?"
So they said to him, "We have not so much as heard
whether there is a Holy Spirit."
[3] And he said to them, "Into what then were you baptized?"
So they said, "Into John's baptism."
[4] Then Paul said, "John indeed baptized with a baptism of
repentance, saying to the people that they should believe on
Him who would come after him, that is, on Christ Jesus."
[5] When they heard this, they were baptized in the name of
the Lord Jesus. [6] And when Paul had laid hands on them,
the Holy Spirit came upon them, and they spoke with
tongues and prophesied.

Acts 19:1-6 NKJV

Now by you receiving the free gift of God's Holy Spirit baptism
and fire, He will give you the divine grace, heavenly wisdom, and
providential anointing you will need to begin and finish your "40-Day
Revival Now Challenge" successfully. At the same time, if you happen
to falter in your fast at any point for any reason, get back up, shake it off,
and continue with your fast as you move ahead with our Lord Jesus
Christ and His Holy Spirit.

Additionally, through the baptism of the Spirit, know He will
help you in your daily life as you continue to pursue Christ, according to
John 14:15-18, 25-26, and John 16:5-14 which say:

[15] If you love Me, keep My commandments. [16] And I will pray
the Father, and He will give you another Helper, that He
may abide with you forever— [17] the Spirit of truth, whom the
world cannot receive, because it neither sees Him nor
knows Him; but you know Him, for He dwells with you and
will be in you. [18] I will not leave you orphans; I will come to
you.

[25]{.superscript} These things I have spoken to you while being present with you. [26]{.superscript} But the Helper, the Holy Spirit, whom the Father will send in My name, He will teach you all things, and bring to your remembrance all things that I said to you.

John 14:15-18, 25-26 NKJV

[5]{.superscript} but now I am going to him who sent me. None of you asks me, 'Where are you going?' [6]{.superscript} Rather, you are filled with grief because I have said these things. [7]{.superscript} But very truly I tell you, it is for your good that I am going away. Unless I go away, the Advocate will not come to you; but if I go, I will send him to you. [8]{.superscript} When he comes, he will prove the world to be in the wrong about sin and righteousness and judgment: [9]{.superscript} about sin, because people do not believe in me; [10]{.superscript} about righteousness, because I am going to the Father, where you can see me no longer; [11]{.superscript} and about judgment, because the prince of this world now stands condemned. [12]{.superscript} I have much more to say to you, more than you can now bear. [13]{.superscript} But when he, the Spirit of truth, comes, he will guide you into all the truth. He will not speak on his own; he will speak only what he hears, and he will tell you what is yet to come. [14]{.superscript} He will glorify me because it is from me that he will receive what he will make known to you.

John 16:5-14 NIV

Lastly, I encourage you to realize that when you are baptized with the Holy Spirit and fire, and are consequently filled with the Holy Spirit, then you will be authorized and empowered by Him to preach the gospel of Jesus Christ with boldness like the Apostle Peter did, according to Acts 4:29-31 which says:

[29]{.superscript} Now, Lord, look on their threats, and grant to Your servants that with all boldness they may speak Your word, [30]{.superscript} by stretching out Your hand to heal, and that signs and

wonders may be done through the name of Your holy Servant Jesus."

31 And when they had prayed, the place where they were assembled together was shaken; and they were all filled with the Holy Spirit, and they spoke the word of God with boldness.

Acts 4:29-31 NKJV

All you have to do is ask our Heavenly Father, in Jesus' name, to give you the gift of His Holy Spirit, according to Luke 11:9-13 which says:

9 So I say to you, ask, and it will be given to you; seek, and you will find; knock, and it will be opened to you. 10 For everyone who asks receives, and he who seeks finds, and to him who knocks it will be opened. 11 If a son asks for bread from any father among you, will he give him a stone? Or if he asks for a fish, will he give him a serpent instead of a fish? 12 Or if he asks for an egg, will he offer him a scorpion? 13 If you then, being evil, know how to give good gifts to your children, how much more will your heavenly Father give the Holy Spirit to those who ask Him!

Luke 11:9-13 NKJV

Now I congratulate and commend you on accepting the "40-Day Revival Now Challenge," and I welcome you to the real remnant of revivalists for revival now. In closing, I extend to you the biblical evangelistic charge from 2 Timothy 4:1-5 which Pastor Matthew Hagee shared with me at Cornerstone Church, on Sunday night, May 5, 2013, when I transitioned with his blessing from the High School Youth Pastor and College and Career Young Adult Pastor roles into evangelism ministry:

¹ I charge you therefore before God and the Lord Jesus Christ, who will judge the living and the dead at His appearing and His kingdom: ² Preach the word! Be ready in season and out of season. Convince, rebuke, exhort, with all longsuffering and teaching. ³ For the time will come when they will not endure sound doctrine, but according to their own desires, because they have itching ears, they will heap up for themselves teachers; ⁴ and they will turn their ears away from the truth, and be turned aside to fables. ⁵ But you be watchful in all things, endure afflictions, do the work of an evangelist, fulfill your ministry.

2 Timothy 4:1-5 NKJV

I received that charge then, and now, I receive it again. Yet this time, I receive it together with you, because it is your time too. Get ready for the next great awakening which will renew our commitment to Christ's Great Commission so the greatest harvest of souls can be brought into God's kingdom before the rapture of the Church and subsequent Great Tribulation occur. History is in the making for the next great awakening, and you and I will be a vital part of it. Let us receive and release revival now, by God's grace, through our Christian faith, and for His glory in Christ Jesus' name. Amen!

Fasting Recommendations: Before you begin your 40-day fast, I highly encourage you to do the following:

1. Consult your doctor for health and nutritional guidance.
2. Consult your pastor for pastoral and spiritual guidance.
3. Conduct your fast with at least one other person, either in your family or church family, since this will provide great support and an exponential impact for you both.
4. Set allowances to your fast, as the Lord leads and gives you the faith, peace, and joy to do so, according to Romans 14:17.

5. Read Christian books on the topic of fasting before or during your fast, such as those authored by Jentezen Franklin and Lou Engle.

ABOUT THE AUTHOR

Peter De Jesús is an ordained minister of Cornerstone Church led by Founding Senior Pastor Dr. John Hagee and Lead Pastor Matthew Hagee, in addition to being a licensed minister of the North Texas District Council of the Assemblies of God led by Superintendent Dr. Gaylan Claunch, Assistant Superintendent Rev. Kermit Bell, and Secretary-Treasurer Rev. Gregg Headley. Peter, together with his wife, Mildred, who is also an NTD AG licensed minister, have been married since 1996. They have served in many ministerial capacities since 1997 including those of youth and young adult, worship, pastoral, evangelistic, and Christian education ministries, in addition to pro-Israel advocacy since 2016. In 2013, they co-founded De Jesús Ministries which ministers bilingually throughout the United States, Puerto Rico, and Central America. Ultimately, their desire is to be ministers of Christ's Kingdom who can be gracefully and powerfully utilized by God to introduce, expand, and advance His heavenly kingdom on earth into the lives of people of all ages all over the world. Peter and Mildred, together with their three children, reside in the Dallas County of Texas, U.S.A.

For more information, visit www.dejesusministries.org. We also invite you to follow Peter on social media platforms:
Facebook: @dejesusministries
Instagram: @revpeterdejesus
Twitter: @pm_dejesus
YouTube: Peter De Jesus

NOTES AND SCRIPTURE CITATIONS

Introduction: My Personal Revival Story

1. Lunar Eclipse, Four Blood Moons, of 2020:
   https://www.google.com/amp/s/www.space.com/amp/33786-lunar-eclipse-guide.html
2. 2 Chronicles 7:13-14 NKJV
3. Mathew 6:33-34 NKJV
4. Matthew 28:18-20 NKJV
5. Luke 21:10-13 NKJV
6. Joel 2:30-32a NKJV
7. Acts 2:19-21 NKJV
8. 1 Kings 19:4 NKJV
9. Isaiah 60:1-2 NKJV
10. Genesis 26:18 NKJV
11. Deuteronomy 9:18 NKJV
12. Romans 8:1 NKJV
13. John 17:20-23 NKJV
14. Luke 22:31-32 NKJV

Chapter 1: What is Revival Now?

1. Acts 2:1-6, 12-21, 37-41 NKJV
2. Acts 2:16 NKJV
3. Joel 2:28-32 NKJV
4. Acts 2:29-33 NKJV
1 Peter 1:16-21 NKJV
5. Acts 1:21-22 NKJV
6. 1 Corinthians 15:3-8 NKJV
7. Acts 5:12 NKJV
8. 2 Corinthians 12:12 NKJV
9. Romans 8:19-22 NKJV

10. Acts 1:8 NKJV
11. Mark 16:15 NKJV
12. Matthew 28:18-20 NKJV
13. Acts 2:41 NKJV
14. Acts 4:4 NKJV
15. Acts 17:26-27 NIV
16. Romans 10:8-9 NKJV
17. John 4:35 NKJV
18. Habakkuk 2:14 NKJV
19. Matthew 24:14 NKJV

Chapter 2: It's Time for a Reality Check

1. 1 Peter 5:8 NKJV
2. John 10:10 NKJV
3. Revelation 5:5 NKJV
4. Ephesians 3:20 NKJV
5. Revelation 3:1-3 NIV
6. Revelation 2:1-5 NKJV
7. Revelation 19:6-9 NIV
8. Revelation 22:17 NKJV
9. John 3:27-30 NKJV
10. Ephesians 5:30-32 NKJV
11. Song of Solomon 8:1-7 NKJV
12. Matthew 25:1-13 NIV
13. Acts 2:1-2 NKJV
14. Acts 2:32-33 NKJV

Chapter 3: There is a Real Remnant

1. Evan Roberts of the 1904 Welsh Revival:
   https://www.christianitytoday.com/history/issues/issue-83/eyewitness.html
2. Acts 2:12-21 NKJV

3. Joel 2:32 NKJV
4. 1 Corinthians 15:3-6 NKJV
5. Acts 1:4, 12-15 NKJV
6. Matthew 14:25-31 NKJV
7. Matthew 16:13-23 NIV
8. Luke 22:29-34, 59-62 NIV
9. John 21:15-17 NKJV
10. Acts 2:40-41 NKJV
11. 1 Peter 2:1-10 NIV
12. Matthew 17:24-27 NKJV
13. Exodus 30:13-14 NKJV
14. Luke 3:23 NKJV
15. Hebrews 12:25-29 NKJV
16. Haggai 2:6-9 NKJV

Chapter 4: The Revolutionary Revelation

1. Acts 2:16-17 NKJV
2. Joel 2:28 NKJV
3. Acts 2:1-6 NKJV
4. Genesis 1:1-5, 11 NKJV
5. Genesis 15:1-6 NKJV
6. Luke 1:26-38 NKJV
7. Proverbs 18:21 NKJV
8. James 3:5-6 NKJV
9. Acts 2:1-4 NKJV
10. Proverbs 29:18 KJV
11. Habakkuk 2:2-3 NKJV
12. Numbers 12:6 NKJV
13. Matthew 1:20 NKJV
14. Mathew 2:13, 19, 22 NKJV

Chapter 5: The Relevant Reasons

1. The Barna Group: https://s3.amazonaws.com/christ-community-church/wp-content/uploads/2019/08/Awana_parent_handbook_2019_20.pdf
2. LifeWay Research: https://lifewayresearch.com/2019/01/15/most-teenagers-drop-out-of-church-as-young-adults/
3. "Resurge" Definition: https://www.dictionary.com/browse/resurge?s=t
4. Romans 13:11 NKJV
5. 2 Corinthians 6:1-2 NKJV
6. Habakkuk 3:1-5 NKJV
7. Psalm 85:4-7 NKJV
8. Mark 10:46-52 NKJV
9. Isaiah 64:6 NKJV
10. Isaiah 57:15 NKJV
11. Ezra 9:8-9 NKJV
12. Luke 19:41-44 NKJV
13. Revelation 3:20-21 NKJV
14. Ephesians 5:14 NKJV
15. Acts 17:26-27 NIV
16. Hosea 6:2 NKJV
17. 2 Peter 3:8 NKJV
18. Ephesians 2:4-6 NKJV
19. Acts 17:26-28 NIV
20. John 12:32 NKJV
21. Mark 9:1-8 NKJV

Chapter 6: The Reverent Rudiments

1. Acts 1:1-8, 12-20 NKJV
2. Acts 2:1 NKJV
3. Psalm 11:3 NKJV
4. Matthew 7:24-29 NKJV
5. Luke 9:23 NKJV

6. 1 Corinthians 15:31 NKJV
7. Galatians 2:20 NKJV
8. Exodus 23:16 NKJV
9. Exodus 34:22 NKJV
10. Numbers 28:26 NKJV
11. Leviticus 23:16 NKJV
12. Ephesians 2:4-7 NKJV
13. Revelation 4:2 NKJV
14. Revelation 1:9-10 NKJV
15. 2 Corinthians 12:1-4 NKJV
16. Revelation 3:21 NKJV
17. Colossians 3:1-4 NKJV
18. Matthew 16:18-19 NKJV

Chapter 7: The Rudiment of Prayer

1. "The Price and Power of Revival" by Duncan Campbell:
    http://articles.ochristian.com/article1650.shtml
2. Acts 1:12-14 NKJV
3. Matthew 6:5-13 NKJV
4. Matthew 26:36-46 NIV
5. Mark 14:32-42 NIV
6. Acts 9:36-42 NKJV
7. 1 Kings 17:17-24 NKJV
8. 2 Kings 4:27-37 NIV
9. James 5:17-18 NKJV
10. Luke 9:28-32 NKJV
11. 2 Chronicles 7:14 NKJV
12. Acts 2:38 NKJV
13. Acts 3:19-21 NKJV
14. 2 Peter 3:9 NKJV
15. Acts 11:17-18 NKJV
16. Acts 17:30-31 NKJV
17. Revelation 3:19 NKJV

18. Matthew 4:17 NKJV
19. Mark 1:14-15 NKJV
20. Luke 13:1-5 NKJV
21. Romans 12:2 NKJV
22. Genesis 18:16-33 NIV
23. Romans 8:26, 34 NKJV
24. Ephesians 6:16 NKJV
25. 1 Corinthians 14:14 NKJV
26. 1 John 5:14-15 NKJV
27. Matthew 6:9-13 NKJV
28. Acts 4:23-31 NKJV

Chapter 8: The Rudiment of Fasting

1. Matthew 6:16-18 NKJV
2. Matthew 9:14-15 NKJV
3. Luke 22:14-19 NKJV
4. Revelation 19:6-9 NKJV
5. Job 23:12 NKJV
6. Isaiah 55:6 NKJV
7. James 4:8 NKJV
8. Isaiah 58:6-8 NKJV
9. Deuteronomy 9:7-29 NIV
10. 1 Kings 19:1-21 NIV
11. Daniel 1:1-21 NIV
12. Esther 4:1-17; 5:1-5 NIV
13. Joel 1:13-15 NIV
14. Joel 2:12-19, 28 NIV
15. Jonah 3:1-10 NIV
16. Luke 4:1-2, 14-21 NIV
17. Mark 9:14-29 NIV
18. Acts 13:1-3 NKJV

Chapter 9: The Rudiment of Worship

1. Leviticus 23:15-22 NKJV
2. Exodus 34:22 NKJV
3. Deuteronomy 16:9-10 NKJV
4. Numbers 28:26 NKJV
5. Genesis 22:1-9 NKJV
6. Psalm 145:3 NKJV
7. 2 Chronicles 5:13-14 NKJV
8. 2 Chronicles 7:1-5 NKJV
9. Romans 12:1 NKJV
10. John 4:23-24 NKJV
11. John 11:1-5, 38-45 NIV
12. John 11:17-37 NIV
13. Luke 10:38-42 NKJV

Chapter 10: The Rudiment of Living According to God's Word

1. Acts 1:15-20 NKJV
2. Acts 2:16-21 NKJV
3. Psalm 119:25, 107 NKJV
4. John 6:63 NKJV
5. Matthew 4:4 NKJV
6. Hebrews 4:12 NKJV
7. 2 Timothy 3:16-17 NKJV
8. Acts 20:7-12 NKJV
9. 2 Corinthians 3:1-3 NKJV
10. John 1:1 NKJV
11. Revelation 19:13 NKJV
12. Luke 8:4-15 NIV
13. Job 23:12 NKJV
14. Matthew 5:18 NKJV
15. 1 Peter 1:22-25 NKJV

Chapter 11: The Rudiment of Unity

1. Acts 1:12-14 NKJV
2. Acts 2:1 NKJV
3. Psalm 133:1-3 NKJV
4. Ephesians 4:1-6 NKJV
5. 1 Corinthians 12:12-27 NIV
6. 1 Corinthians 1:10-13 NKJV
7. John 17:20-23 NKJV
8. John 21:1-7, 15-17 NKJV
9. Acts 2:41-47 NKJV
10. 1 Kings 18:36-46 NIV
11. 1 Kings 19:1-18 NIV
12. Acts 1:12-14 NKJV
13. Acts 2:1-4 NKJV
14. Matthew 16:13-23 NKJV
15. Luke 22:28-34, 54-62 NKJV
16. Matthew 18:6 NKJV
17. Mark 9:42 NKJV
18. Luke 17:1-2 NKJV
19. Matthew 18:18-20 NKJV
20. Matthew 27:1-5 NKJV
21. Acts 1:15-20 NKJV
22. Acts 2:14-16 NKJV
23. 1 Corinthians 11:17-34 NIV
24. 2 Corinthians 5:18-21 NKJV
25. Revelation 5:5-10 NIV
26. Revelation 7:9-10 NIV

Chapter 12: It's Time to Recruit Revivalists Now!

1. Ephesians 5:14 NKJV
2. John 4:39-42 NKJV
3. John 12:9-11 NKJV
4. Ezekiel 37:1-10 NIV

5. Acts 2:38-41 NKJV
6. Acts 4:4 NKJV
7. Acts 17:5-6 NKJV
8. Ephesians 5:15-17 NKJV
9. Acts 2:1-4 NKJV
10. Luke 3:16 NKJV
11. Luke 12:49 NKJV
12. Acts 1:4-5 NKJV
13. Acts 9:17-18 NKJV
14. Acts 10:44-45 NKJV
15. Acts 19:1-6 NKJV
16. John 14:15-18, 25-26 NKJV
17. John 16:5-14 NIV
18. Luke 11:9-13 NKJV
19. Acts 4:29-31 NKJV
20. 2 Timothy 4:1-5 NKJV